Preparing for the Glory

John and Carol Arnott care intensely about the subject of preparing for a move of God. Revival has two key elements. There is the sovereign, "suddenly" aspect where it seems God hits a community like lightning. Unexpected and dramatic. And yet, it's also possible to prepare for it. When you study the climate leading up to the "suddenlies" of God, you notice some common denominators—some preparatory elements that, no doubt, readied the atmosphere and the people for an invasion of God's Spirit.

Preparing for the Glory is more than another book on Holy Spirit outpouring or revival, it's an exhortation for people to prepare for a wave of the Spirit. While the planet grows darker, Scripture makes a compelling case that the glory of God will increase upon the people of God (see Isaiah 60:1-2). God's glory will be released, brighter and brighter, through a community of people who are longing to express His glory in the darkness. This glory will look like signs and wonders that point many to Jesus. It will look like unusual manifestations that direct people to the living God. It will look like a return of the fear of the Lord to a generation that has, perhaps, gotten a little too comfortable with the One who should be awed and revered.

I appreciate this book because I so appreciate John and Carol. I know them. I know their lives. What you are receiving in book form is a simple, practical, but very powerful behind-the-scenes look into how these two leaders prepared for and stewarded a "lightning strike" of the Lord back in 1994 when the Holy Spirit impacted the world through the Toronto Blessing. But don't be fooled. This book is not a rehash of the "good ole days." More than revival stories, the

Arnotts give you transferable principles that you can apply to your own life to experience personal renewal—at an individual level. On a corporate level, this is a book that will help prepare pastors, leaders, and church communities to position themselves for a wave of the Holy Spirit.

The Arnotts have written this book with their lives, and I believe it will inspire a fresh hunger in you to pursue and experience the glory of God like never before!

MIKE BICKLE
International House of Prayer, Kansas City MO
Bestselling author of *Growing in the Prophetic* and
Growing in Prayer

John and Carol Arnott know revival. But the next tsunami will be the mother of all revivals. Many will be put on the shelf because they did not heed the prophetic warning. The best is yet to come!

SID ROTH,
Host, *It's Supernatural!*

When I think of John and Carol Arnott, I think of revival. They are pioneers of the modern-day outpourings, which have touched the nations. As I read the manuscript for their latest book, *Preparing for the Glory*, I found myself yearning for whatever Holy Spirit is conditioning us for. I have often said that once you put your feet under the table of revival, no other table will ever satisfy. The Arnotts brought us to the table for the first move, and it is evident they will lead the way to help bring us to the greatest glory yet to be revealed.

JOHN A. KILPATRICK
Founder and Senior Pastor, Church of His Presence

Three months before the Brownsville Revival began, I wrote a book that ended with the words, "Are you ready?" Now John and Carol Arnott, who have been champions of revival and renewal for the last twenty-five years, are asking that same question again: Are we ready for a greater wave of revival than any of us have ever experienced? The Arnott's predict that a holy tsunami is coming, and this book will help prepare the way.

DR. MICHAEL L. BROWN

President, FIRE School of Ministry

Author of *Whatever Happened to the Power of God*,

From Holy Laughter to Holy Fire, Authentic Fire

and co-author of *The Fire That Never Sleeps*

John and Carol Arnott will go down as two of the most extraordinary servants of God in the history of the Christian church. If Jesus tarries, historians will record the phenomenon that took place in the Toronto Vineyard Fellowship in 1994 as the beginning of an outpouring of the Holy Spirit that literally swept the entire globe. Many of the severest critics—whether theologians or sociologists—have had eventually to affirm this surprising event as a positive movement that changed churches generally and individuals particularly. My former church in London—Westminster Chapel—and I myself—became a part of this.

The big thing is this—it is very simple: I will have to stand before God one day and give an account of my decisions. That is enough to solidify me in my endorsement of the Toronto Blessing and the honesty of John and Carol. Yes, it is His opinion that matters.

RT Kendall

Bestselling author of *Total Forgiveness*,

The Anointing, and *Holy Fire*

"For the earth will be filled with the knowledge of the glory of the Lord, as the waters cover the sea" (Habakkuk 2:14). *Preparing for the Glory* is a significant book by my longtime, good friends

John and Carol Arnott, enticing us for not only more of the Holy Spirit, but also a greater wave of revival than we have already witnessed. John and Carol reflect on the powerful move of the Spirit that was called the "Toronto Blessing," to remind us that a great outpouring of revival didn't happen by accident—it was a fruit of spiritual hunger and preparation.

As Jesus instructed in Matthew 9, no one puts new wine in old wineskins, because the wineskin would break and the wine would be spilled. A new wineskin—built upon encountering Love in the person of the Holy Spirit and intimacy with Jesus—made space for the new wine to be wonderfully poured out in the Toronto blessing. *Preparing for the Glory* begs the question, "Are we ready?" for the next outpouring, the greater wave of revival that is already building, as God is moving tremendously across the nations today.

We are given a gift in this book forged through the first-hand experience of John and Carol, my fellow members of Revival Alliance, encouraging us that *there is more,* as the signs of shifting and a tsunami-sized wave of revival are beginning to show throughout the earth and the time for preparations are at hand. *Preparing for the Glory* stirs our hearts to remember that revival is ours for the taking, as the Lord is calling us to, "Get ready, get ready, get ready."

Dr. Ché Ahn
President, Harvest International Ministry
Founding Pastor, HROCK Church, Pasadena, CA
International Chancellor, Wagner University

Like countless thousands of others, I have known of John and Carol Arnott for years. I actually "met" them in a dream before the Toronto Outpouring in 1994. In my dream, John was prophesying to me about the future in which I am now walking. This was before I knew anyone named Arnott, yet I knew the man speaking to me had that name. My wife, Mary, a team from our church, and I went to Toronto six months into the outpouring when the world began to know the Arnott name. We were dramatically impacted. Everything changed in our ministry and life. This is one of the reasons I am excited about this new book.

Another generation of believers has the opportunity to learn the history of revival, but also to prepare for its future! John and Carol's book, *Preparing for the Glory,* is a prophetic declaration of God's intentions in the earth. As generals chosen and empowered to steward the revival of God in the earth, John and Carol give clear prophetic insight. They stir us again to hunger and desire Jesus more. They, however, also give us a pattern for seeing God's presence come in more powerful waves of His glory. Remember, Jesus said in John 7:38 that there were "rivers" of His glory. Let's take the limits off and allow God to shape us through even more encounters with Him. The future belongs to those empowered by the unrestrained glory of God. They will be used to bring honor to the King.

ROBERT HENDERSON
Robert Henderson Ministries
Bestselling author of *Operating in the Courts of Heaven*

The outpouring of the Spirit in Toronto that began on January 20, 2014, was and is an historical event that came right out of Heaven. I flew our team out to Toronto many times a year in those early days to drink of the glory of God—and did we ever get FILLED! There was always MORE for everyone who was hungry; and the hungry converged from all around the world. One of the amazing things I noted was that most of those who were in the outpouring would return to their homes and it would break out there as well.

The manifestations of the Spirit in the Toronto Blessing were outrageous, authentic, controversial, and life-transforming. With so many unique and sovereign manifestations of grace, it required great stewardship; and for that purpose, my attention was on John and Carol Arnott as I observed them nurture, steward, and protect with amazing Spirit-led freedom this amazing move of God. If God were to give grades for stewardship, they would receive an A+ for sure!

My life was deeply and profoundly impacted through those many years of outpouring. How wonderful and gracious is our God! I am forever grateful.

DR. PATRICIA KING
Founder, Patricia King Ministries
www.patriciaking.com

The Toronto Blessing was one of the most unique and powerful moves of God of the 20th century. Thousands from all around the world came to experience it, and left spreading the fire to the corners of the earth. As I crisscrossed the world speaking to churches and conferences, there was a period of several years when I did not go anywhere that I did not see the impact of "the blessing." When I did, I knew I was with people who loved the Holy Spirit and His works, and God would do great things among them. Now, John and Carol Arnott, great examples of hosts of the Holy Spirit, have written this book that is also unique. It is a history, a teaching, an apologetic, and a prophecy all wrapped into one—and it will help prepare the way for the Lord's next great move.

RICK JOYNER
Senior Leader and Founder,
MorningStar Ministries, Fort Mill, SC
Bestselling author of *The Final Quest*

PREPARING
for the
GLORY

OTHER BOOKS BY JOHN AND CAROL ARNOTT

Manifestations and Prophetic Symbolism

From Here to the Nations: The Story of the Toronto Blessing

The Invitation

Grace and Forgiveness

Experience the Blessing

PREPARING
for the
GLORY

*Getting Ready for the Next Wave
of Holy Spirit Outpouring*

JOHN & CAROL ARNOTT

DESTINY IMAGE® PUBLISHERS, INC.

P.O. Box 310, Shippensburg, PA 17257-0310

"Promoting Inspired Lives."

This book and all other Destiny Image and Destiny Image Fiction books are available at Christian bookstores and distributors worldwide.

For more information on foreign distributors, call 717-532-3040.

Reach us on the Internet: www.destinyimage.com.

Interior design by Terry Clifton

ISBN 13 TP: 978-0-7684-1787-6
ISBN 13 eBook: 978-0-7684-1788-3
ISBN 13 HC: 978-0-7684-1790-6
ISBN 13 LP: 978-0-7684-1789-0

For Worldwide Distribution, Printed in the U.S.A.
1 2 3 4 5 6 7 8 / 22 21 20 19 18

We dedicate this book to the precious Holy Spirit. How faithful He has been to us all of these years!

And yet, with all we have seen and experienced, we pray once again. We pray for a new generation, and for a great increase in His power and manifest presence for this most urgent hour—come even more Holy Spirit.

Acknowledgments

WE WANT TO SPECIFICALLY THANK THE CHURCH FAMILY AND leadership of Catch the Fire Toronto (Formerly, Toronto Airport Christian Fellowship). This wonderful outpouring that we have been enjoying since 1994 is because of your stewardship in the local church and your commitment to serve the nations.

May His glory continue to fall upon you, as you've consistently proven your trustworthiness to release it to the nations.

Thanks to Nancy Smith, Larry Sparks, and the team at Destiny Image for making this book possible.

Contents

Foreword

DO YOU WANT REVIVAL? DO YOU WANT GOD TO POUR OUT HIS glory and transform your family, your city, your nation? God wants that too! At the center of everything is the greatest love story of all time where Jesus pursues His Bride, and we respond. Personally and corporately, our focus must be on our own love for Jesus and on His deep love for the lost. This love sparks hunger in us for God and for His Kingdom to come on earth, for revival to break forth. Love makes us want more of His presence. Love bubbles over, and we can't help but tell people about the One we love. We begin to feel God's heart for people, and we are filled with compassion for their situations. We get filled with faith knowing God wants to heal them, bring their breakthroughs, and make Himself known in tangible ways. Love makes us want revival—an awakening of whole communities to see who God is and to fall in love with Jesus.

As we pray for revival, there are practical things we can do to position ourselves and our churches. One of the ways we can prepare is by studying other revivals. John and Carol Arnott have written this incredible book, *Preparing for the Glory*, about their personal journey in God and about the Toronto Blessing, a powerful revival that began at their church in 1994. The book details their pursuit for revival then and now. They also share their research on historical revivals and on anointed men and women of God who taught them along the way. In each revival, there is a particular aspect of God that He wants to reveal to the Church. It is important to look for what God is highlighting in each great movement. We want to learn and receive everything He is revealing to us!

John and Carol have found tools and keys that they share throughout the book. They give us practical things that have helped them and many others in their church to have encounters with God and grow in intimacy with Him. God loves when we "tarry" in His presence through soaking, worship, and reading His Word. Being intentional with our time is a huge key to seeing revival. God also loves when we release our need for control and allow Him to do whatever He wants in and through us. Even if we fall over or look strange, He wants us to be willing to be filled by Him, no matter the cost. God loves us, so He wants to be with us. He wants us to focus our attention on Him and to position our lives toward Him. In doing this, we make ourselves ready for revival.

In addition to preparing individually, we need to be part of a community with the same passion for God. John, Carol, Rolland, and I and a small group of other leaders formed the Revival Alliance, a group set on meeting together to pray for and pursue revival. We meet together each year and host conferences to corporately ask God what He wants to do in our generation and position ourselves and our movements for more of Him. Unity is another crucial key for revival, so part of the purpose of Revival Alliance is to bring our movements together. We have different specific missions and characteristics but the same Father, the same passion for Christ, and the same Holy Spirit. We cheer each other on in our victories and encourage each other when we go through challenging times.

I urge you to meet with others who have similar hearts and who also want more of God in your locality. God created us for family and community! John and Carol also encourage spending time visiting places, experiencing revival, and asking God to give you a personal encounter. You are welcome to apply to come visit Mozambique. We would love to have you come and participate in what God is doing and experience more of Him. I'm sure John and Carol would welcome you to come visit Toronto and pray for God to meet you there. Myself and countless others have had life-changing encounters on that carpet; it is a very special place.

John and Carol and their teams have received many prophetic words and dreams for the next wave of revival. They are actively praying for this and seeing it. They sense that God wants to release a revival of holiness. Holiness is something that many have misunderstood or pushed aside. Our culture and society are fighting hard against us in this regard, tempting individuals and communities worldwide with compromises and gray areas. Certain movements in the church have even believed the lie that grace is freely available so we can do whatever we please and our sins don't really matter. True grace actually empowers us to live holy lives. The more we fall in love with Jesus, the more we want our lives to please His heart. We want to be like Him; we do not want any compromise or any areas that His light hasn't touched in our hearts.

We want to give everything to the One we love; we want every word, every action, every decision to please His heart because of love. Holiness is not a burden or a chore; it becomes our joy.

John and Carol are the perfect people to share with us about what it looks like and what it feels like to see revival, both how to prepare and how to respond. Even after experiencing so much in God and hosting one of the most impactful revivals in our generation, they are continuously preparing themselves and their church for another, greater wave. John and Carol are passionate people who have no intention of stopping or settling. They know full well that there is always more. It is a great privilege and honor to count them as some of my closest friends. Jesus says we will do greater things than He did. Most of us have not seen or experienced that yet, but we want to, and we know that everything He says is true.

Jesus is so in love with you. He wants more of you; do you want more of Him? I encourage you to read this book and allow God to stir up more hunger in you for revival. I have personally been impacted by the Lord in this revival in a way that has caused me to fall more in love with Jesus and courageously pursue His purposes in my life, to find the lost and the broken and bring them home to Jesus and the Father. I pray that you will also be transformed forever as you allow Him to encounter you and fill you to overflowing. He has amazing things for you and for your community beyond what you could ask or imagine. So you better *Prepare for the Glory.* because it is coming!

HEIDI G. BAKER, PHD
Co-founder and CEO of Iris Global
Bestselling author of *Birthing the Miraculous*

Introduction

Bill Johnson

BENI AND I ATTENDED THE 20-YEAR ANNIVERSARY OF THE TORONTO outpouring. It was a gathering of many of our heroes of the faith who are alive today, plus thousands of people I had never met before. They were there to give honor to God for all He had done and bring their deepest cry to God for the "more" that He has promised. If there's anything this movement is known for, it is hunger for more.

Each person at the event had a different story. The Father's Blessing, as it became affectionately called, had impacted us all in different ways. Countless marriages were healed. People came sick and diseased and left healed. Skeptics came to mock and left with the unquestionable realization that God was real and He was good. And now they knew why they were alive. Many lost people also attended and came to faith in Christ.

This outpouring seemed to have a special effect on pastors who had come as a last stop before quitting the ministry altogether. Numerous leaders left refreshed, and in many ways "retooled" for the days directly ahead of them. It has been a most wonderful thing to observe that in that manifested presence of God's glory, any need could be met.

My Story

My story was a bit different. I wasn't a burnt-out pastor, nor was I wanting to quit. It was quite the opposite. I came to Toronto in a very good place. But it was also true that I lived with an awareness of more, and would pay any price to get it. It had been reported to me that God was doing great things there, so I went.

My hunger for all that God was doing was in part the result of reading of past revivals, knowing I was born for such a thing. It was also a product of the environment I was raised in. Great outpourings of the Spirit were part of our family's history. Some of my family members were involved in the Azusa Street revival of the early 1900s, while others were part of the ministry of Aimee Semple McPherson and/or Smith Wigglesworth. And still others were involved in other moves of God that were not as well known.

My grandfather loved to talk to me about what he had seen happen in his lifetime. He experienced the baptism in the Holy Spirit in 1901, and my grandmother in 1903. That experience created quite a stir in the church of his day. He was also one who sat under Smith Wigglesworth's ministry. In fact, my aunt and others received the baptism of the Holy Spirit in his meetings.

But my grandfather also told me that not everyone liked Smith Wigglesworth. His extreme faith made people nervous. Of course, we love him today, because he's dead. Israel also loved all their dead prophets too, after their controversy wore off. It's the leaders who are alive who often lead us into unfamiliar territory, that we have the most trouble with. Realizing that helps me to deal with the opposition we receive today, often from well-meaning believers.

Unfamiliar Manifestations

There were many things happening in the Toronto meetings I had not seen before, but they were consistent with the stories passed down from our family. It was different, and it required that I make some adjustments to my thinking. But hunger makes change easy. In the same way that a truly starving person doesn't send the meat back to the chef because the he wanted it medium, not medium rare, so the hunger for more of God at any cost makes gratefulness the driving response to anything He does.

My first trip to Toronto was in February 1995. The revival had been underway for 13 months by that time, and they had learned a bit about stewarding a move of God. It was fascinating to watch, as they carefully navigated the journey of doing what the Father was doing without falling into the trap of trying to control the Holy Spirit out of a fear of what people might think. If there was ever a group that did that well, it was

John and Carol and their team of leaders. I was stunned and still am to this day. I don't know anyone who navigates that challenge better.

On my way to Toronto I prayed a simple prayer, "God, if You will touch me again, I'll never change the subject." I had attended two John Wimber conferences in 1987 that had great impact on my life. Breakthroughs in the miraculous started to manifest immediately. Many of those *outbreaks* of God I had never seen before. While I loved what God was doing, I didn't know how to sustain what God had given me. It wasn't a fear of man, nor was it an unwillingness to "bend with God." I just didn't know what to do. I didn't know that it was God who lit the fire on the altar—but it was the priests who kept it burning.

This time I asked God to touch me again, and I'd do whatever needed to be done to keep it burning. *Never changing the subject* for me meant I wouldn't add what He was doing to what we were doing. I would make His outpouring the only thing I would give myself to.

While I didn't have any dramatic experiences that week in Toronto like the things I watched happen to many others around me, I was profoundly impacted. As a result, I committed myself completely to this movement.

Upon returning home, this wonderful outpouring of the Holy Spirit came to us as well. We would never be the same.

It's Time for Offense

Moves of God always contain something different and something offensive. It seems to be the way He moves. This time the laughter (joy) as well as the focus on getting blessed were highly criticized in much the same way that tongues were criticized in the early 1900s. Saying yes to this journey helped me to discover that joy was to salvation what tears were to repentance. Suddenly the offensive became rather logical.

I, along with my dad, brother, and brother-in-law, visited my grandmother in a nursing home in the Midwest. She was 97. She wanted to know what God was doing among us, so I told her. She listened with great excitement as she loved the moves of God with all her heart. When I mentioned the *joy* part of the equation, she got a stern look on her face, looked me in the eye and said, "You know that's from God, don't you?" I laughed and told her yes. She was relieved. She wanted to make sure I didn't reject it just because it caused offense.

Twenty Years in Review

During the 20-year anniversary celebration, we were able to see more clearly what had happened over the previous 20 years. The reports came in by the droves. It was astounding. Tens of thousands of churches had been planted. Millions and millions of people have come to Christ. Many missionaries have been released into the darkest parts of the world. Signs and wonders have become more normal, as God's people have become better equipped to display this gospel with the power needed for a miracle. The very things that were criticisms of this revival were used to bring forth its most pronounced fruit. Only God could bring about the conversion of millions of souls by giving broken people joy. Only God could have spiritual leaders finally receive for themselves without shame. It was beautiful to see the Lord then turn their blessing around and make them a blessing, using them in miracles, signs, and wonders. This is truly the Lord's doing, and it is wonderful.

It was only after my first two visits to Toronto that Beni and I became friends with John and Carol and their wonderful team. They have been to Redding many times, and in turn it has been my privilege to speak at a number of their conferences. I don't think I've ever missed the chance to express my somewhat humorous thanks for the chance to be back on the "mother ship" before I brought the message. Because of the privilege of being one of the speakers, I've had the thrill of sitting next to John and Carol on the front row during countless meetings. I've never left those times without the intense desire to be more like the Jesus I see in them as they celebrate every little thing that He does among them. It remains a mystery to me how anyone who has seen as much as those two have, can maintain such a childlike approach to all that God is doing among them. Their gratefulness is contagious.

My experience on the front row with John and Carol goes something like this: Someone will be brought to the stage to give a testimony of what God has done for them. Carol will lean over to John and say, "Isn't that wonderful, John?" And he'll respond, "It is Carol, it is." And it truly is. But here's the backstory. What they just heard in that testimony is something they've heard hundreds of times before, literally. And yet the simple thanks and celebration for anything that God is doing remains genuine, childlike, and constant. I sit there stunned every single time.

I now anticipate the opportunity to have my world rocked again by being with them. It appears to me that perhaps the heart of a child, that they have so masterfully maintained, is the reason God has entrusted them with so much. They truly steward a move of God unlike anyone I know or anyone I've ever read about in church history. Should the Lord not return for another 30 years or so, I believe that what we've witnessed in Toronto, and now all over the world, will go down in history as the greatest move of God to date. I say that without hesitation as it pertains to the past. But I say it with reservation as it pertains to our immediate future. For it is the conviction of us all that we are on the edge of what will be the greatest revival in all of history. In fact, I sincerely believe that this next outpouring of the Spirit will contain all the elements of every true move of God of the past, combined into one explosive outpouring for the harvest of souls and nations.

Preparing for the Glory!

Our 20-year celebration was for this purpose: we gave thanks for the past while pressing ahead into all that God has promised, for this is to be the greatest hour in history. *Preparing for the Glory* was written entirely for this reason—to launch us into a fresh hunger and passion for all that God has promised. And I believe that God will use the book to ignite the hearts of countless numbers of believers to hunger once again, with a willingness to pay any price, and that God would once again surpass all we could ask or think, all to His glory.

Chapter 1

A Prophetic Journey

For the Lord would say this is not just an anniversary; it is a sign and a wonder—a sign for what God is getting ready to release and a wonder as it marks the releasing of a new move of the Holy Spirit that is the marriage of both wind and fire.

This is not only the time to look back but to be propelled forward! I am going to do double what I have done with you as a couple and double what I did in the last visitation, says the Lord.

This is the day of the Elisha Awakening.
—CINDY JACOBS, January 14, 2014

IN JANUARY 2014, THOUSANDS OF PEOPLE GATHERED TO CELE-BRATE what had become known as the "Toronto Blessing," which had begun 20 years earlier on a cold Thursday night in 1994. That original meeting was comprised of about 120 people and a relatively unknown speaker by the name of Randy Clark. During the meeting, Randy shared his testimony—and kaboom! The Holy Spirit fell on all those in the room. And the rest, as they say, is history.

Twenty years later, on a much colder night in a much larger room, thousands gathered to not just remember that time but to look forward to what God was up to next. Many in the room were part of those early days: Randy Clark and his wife DeAnne were in attendance, as were Bill and Beni Johnson of Bethel Church in Redding, California; Rolland and Heidi Baker of IRIS Global; Ché and Sue Ahn, founders of HRock Church in Los Angeles; and Georgian and Winnie Banov, founders of Global Celebration Ministries—all leaders of the Revival Alliance, a group dedicated to the spread of revival on the earth and who had all had their lives changed by coming to Toronto. Some others were there who had been touched by the revival even though they themselves had never been to Toronto before. The atmosphere was electric.

A "wave" of revival, many had called it. "The river," others said. Habakkuk 2:14 says, *"For the earth will be filled with the knowledge of the glory of the Lord, as the waters cover the sea."* For 20 years, millions of people from every corner of the planet had come to dive deep into the presence of the Holy Spirit, to immerse themselves in His love. The waters were spreading.

But on that 20th anniversary, we knew there was more. There was always more. In 1998, I (John) had a dream about a massive tsunami-like wave that nothing could stop. At the time, I thought it was symbolic of the revival we were already seeing. At that point, we were meeting six nights a week (we took Mondays off), and thousands upon thousands were being touched by what was happening. In the ensuing years, we would see millions of people pass through our doors, and we saw miracle upon miracle as many were touched and healed by the Father's love in their bodies and minds and hearts. It felt like a pretty big wave.

But as we prepared for the anniversary celebration in early January 2014, we knew we hadn't seen the fullness of that enormous wave—yet. Around January 10, our personal assistant Ruth Preston came to us with a dream she had had. Ruth and her husband, Marcel, serve at Catch the Fire in many ways, including pastoring our central campus in downtown Toronto as well as being powerfully anointed worship leaders whose music is igniting hearts around the world. Well, Ruth shared with us her dream—about a wave. In her words:

> I had this dream on repeat all night. I must have dreamed it anywhere from 15 to 30 times...I saw a picture of a large tidal wave (like a tsunami wave) coming in toward the shore. It was displacing the water in front of it so that it looked as if it was pushing another smaller wave in front. Then, a medium-sized wave came up from the shore toward the big wave. When they met, they crashed together and went straight up into the air. Then each wave went backward partially. Some of the water went straight down to create what looked like a swirling water heart. The water swirled at the bottom moving, moving, moving, and then I heard the Lord speak a word that was then physically stamped over the heart. The word changed throughout the dream sequence. It was alternately, "Compelled," "Championed," "Christ," and "Compassion."

A bigger wave was coming. Is coming. We see it; we know that what began all those years ago was just the beginning. You see, as good as the past 20-plus years have been, we are not satisfied. We want more.

And it seems that God does, too. In the weeks and months leading up to the 2014 conference, we received many prophetic words confirming that God isn't finished with us yet, that what He began on that Thursday night in 1994 was just the smaller wave.

The bigger wave is coming.

In 1993, our friend Stacey Campbell prophesied, "The Lord is going to come in a wave of miracles...And it (will go) not only from this place, from the interior of this province, but it (will) go from nation to nation to nation to nation." During the first night of our anniversary celebration, Stacey prophesied again:

> The Lord told me when I was 27 [20 years earlier] it would not be our generation but would be the generation behind us. That they would do signs, they would do wonders, and they would change nations... A wave of My holiness, a wave of My power, My reformation power, is coming to this nation and many other nations too. Because the low places will be made high, the high places will be made low for that generation who prepares the way for the coming of the Lord.

Now, Stacey has been with us many times over the years. She knows very well that the wave of miracles indeed came to Toronto—and went out from us to many, many nations. But the Lord has more. He always has more. And like Moses hidden in the cleft of the rock, we have only just begun to see His glory.

In 2013, Patricia King shared with us that back in 1980 she had been given a vision from the Lord of a tsunami-like wave—and that He had now given her a vision of a "monster wave": "A move is coming—the greatest move ever is going to come suddenly, like a monster wave. It will be different from the ones in the past. It's always different than you expect, but better. It will be a holiness revival."

It's happening. We saw it recently in our church in Iceland, and in our church in New Zealand. Our friend Ken Gott was just in Hawaii, and had a meeting where the presence of God was evident in a way he said he hadn't seen since the mid-90s. We're seeing the fingerprints of God in places like Raleigh, North Carolina; London, England; all over Canada—all over the world. It's like God is saying to us, "I'm telling you, I'm doing it. I'm doing it." He has been moving all along but is moving now at a much greater intensity.

> When the Holy Spirit fell in 1994, I asked God what He was doing. Instead of explaining Himself, He just said, "I am going easy on you now so you won't be totally shocked and terrified when the real power shows up."

In fact, Barbara Yoder prophesied that the wave would be so massive, we won't be able to swim in it; we'll be carried along to places we've never been able to go before. She said that this next wave would propel us into the deeper places.

When the Holy Spirit fell in 1994, I asked God what He was doing. Instead of explaining Himself, He just said, "I am going easy on you now so you won't be totally shocked and terrified when the real power shows up."

The real power. In other words, we haven't seen anything yet. God has greater glory to release on the earth than we've ever seen before.

Revival didn't come to Toronto by accident, though. Although it seemed to be "sudden," it wasn't sudden to God at all—and it wasn't really sudden to us. We had been preparing, crying out, seeking, and hungering for revival for many, many years. In many ways, the outpouring of the Spirit in 1994 was the result of preparations God had been asking us to make for a long time. You see, wine needs a container. If the wine begins to pour out before the container is ready for it, you just have a big mess. The purpose of this book is to tell a bit of our story, along with what God has shown us in the past 20 or so years, to help us as the Church prepare for the next big wave.

There has been a historical tendency for leaders of one revival to be the first to criticize the next wave of revival. To that we say, "Help me, Jesus." We are privileged to have raised up spiritual sons and daughters who are taking up the mantle of revival and will ride the next wave of glory. We pray that they would exceed our thresholds, going deeper and farther than we ever thought possible. We know that this next wave will look different; but it will look like God. It will look like His glory. We're ready.

Are you?

Chapter 2

The Hunger

*Oh, taste and see that the Lord is good; blessed
is the man who trusts in Him!*

—Psalm 34:8

Have you ever been hungry? Maybe it's been a while since
you last ate, and your stomach is grumbling. Your pizza from
last night is long gone, and you forgot to eat breakfast. Rumble, rumble, it goes. And it's all you can think about; you just
can't wait for lunch. You just can't wait to taste food again.
Maybe you start imagining what you're going to eat—what
it will look like, what it will smell like, what it will taste like.
You can almost taste it now. In your lunch bag is your favorite sandwich, or maybe you're going out to lunch at a favorite
restaurant for a coworker's birthday, and just for a minute you
savor the thought of fulfilling that hunger. Your mouth even
starts to water just a little bit...and then, finally, you get to eat

it. You eat your sandwich, or your favorite food at your favorite restaurant, and it is delicious. The taste reminds you all over again why it's your favorite, and even after you're done, you know you're going to have to eat it again—and soon.

Taste and See

The Lord asks us to "taste and see" that He is good. He wants us to hunger for Him and His presence more than we would hunger for anything else in the world. And just like your favorite food, when you get a little bit of Him, He knows that you're just going to want more. Unlike the food we eat, there is never too much of God. We can never consume too much of Him, of His presence, of His goodness. We could taste of His love forever and ever, and we would never get enough.

> The Lord asks us to "taste and see" that He is good. He wants us to hunger for Him and His presence more than we would hunger for anything else in the world.

We began our journey with a hunger. What happened on that night in 1994 was what we had been longing for, for a very long time. We had been in business for a while, with John running a travel agency. But we began to see a deep need in the church to see people really being helped and really being discipled. We had seen so many come to church, attend for a while, and then fall away. And it wasn't just the church we attended; we knew so many others who were having the same experience.

Even then, we wanted more.

Beginnings in Stratford

We left our businesses in 1981 and started a church in Carol's hometown of Stratford. Right away we had a harvest of many, many young people. There were about a hundred and fifty of them, and they were very broken in so many ways. Broken homes, broken marriages, broken souls—they were disappointed and disillusioned. Nobody comes from a perfect background, but even our history of divorce and remarriage looked fairly healthy by comparison. The things these people had been through were absolutely heartbreaking, and we were desperate to help.

We began to ask, "God, how do we help these people?" Our old model of, "Just read the Bible, do what it says, and you'll be fine," wasn't working anymore. They needed more.

Encounter with Love

We began to realize that what these hurting and broken young people needed was an encounter with love. Not the worldly kind, where it's all about getting your needs met and having a good time. No, what these folks needed was an encounter with Love Himself, in the person of the Holy Spirit. They needed His touch to penetrate their hearts, igniting a romance like they had never experienced before. They needed true Love to come in and spark desire for God, desire for His presence, desire for intimacy with Him. It seemed to be that when they had genuinely encountered His presence and been deeply touched, they would make it. That was the main thing that brought about real change—all the self-discipline, pull-yourself-up-by-your-bootstraps thinking we had tried in the past didn't help.

The more we watched the Holy Spirit at work in this way, the more we were sold on the presence and the power of the Holy Spirit as the only real way to transform lives. And the more we saw of it, the more we wanted.

That's hunger.

Seeing More

Once you begin to see lives really changed and hearts truly healed, you will do whatever it takes to have more of it. We asked God to show us how we could see the more we so desperately wanted.

As a younger man, I (John) had attended many Kathryn Kuhlman meetings. While of course Jesus is my rescuer, watching the Holy Spirit at work in those meetings had rescued me from a certain level of cynicism. The way she ministered just felt so normal, and then miracles would begin to happen. Words of knowledge, healings, more of the supernatural than I had ever thought possible. She influenced an entire generation, myself included, to think that God is real and God is wonderful and He does miracles. We saw them, right in front of us.

We have known Benny Hinn for years and watched as God began to move powerfully in Benny's meetings. In 1992, we again attended his meeting ourselves. In that meeting we saw the lame walk and the blind see and the deaf hear, and about a thousand people came to Christ. Carol got so undone by the Holy Spirit, I had to carry her home. She was heavy under the weight of God's glory and could barely walk.

As I (John) carried her, I told her, "Don't try to get it together, babe. Just stay under this. This is what we want. Just go with it; I'll get you home. Don't worry. Just stay there."

I (Carol) was buzzing. Electrified. And I knew we had to have more of this. We were staying with Jeremy and Connie Sinnott, friends of ours in Toronto. We got back to their house that night, and we said to the Lord, "We have to have this." I knew I couldn't do ministry anymore without what I had experienced that night. The hunger that had begun years ago had now become ravenous—I needed *more*.

As we cried out to the Lord that night, He answered us. He said, "If you're serious, I'll give you two things to do. Number one, I want your mornings. And number two, I want you to hang around people who are anointed."

> You don't give up on a marriage because you don't "feel" something one day; neither do you give up on Jesus because you didn't "feel" something during your quiet time.

So we did. We gave God our mornings; we committed to spending time with Him before anything else. I clearly understood the first of those two things, but not so much the second one. I realize now that He was speaking about impartation.

Sometimes, our morning time looked like radical encounters where we felt His presence very strongly; other times, it looked like reading chapters and chapters of the Bible. We worshiped and soaked in His presence. Some mornings would be glorious. Sometimes, it looked like holding to our commitment to Him—even when we didn't feel much.

Carol's experience at Benny's meeting had been so powerful, and I think in some sense we had thought that our time with Him would always be like that. But some mornings, it was just getting up, having our coffee, worshiping or reading the Bible, and knowing that no matter what we felt—or didn't feel—that He was with us. And it was always good.

It's About Love

So many have accused us over the years of being all about the "experience." And of course we love to have powerful experiences with God. Why wouldn't we? But what had begun to stir in us was a love affair with Jesus, not merely a one-time encounter. And love affairs have days that are emotional and romantic and wonderful and other days that are quiet and unremarkable. You don't give up on a marriage because you don't "feel" something one day; neither do you give up on Jesus because you didn't "feel" something during your quiet time.

You see, we were learning to fall in love with Jesus at a deeper level. Twenty years previously, I had had a powerful encounter with the love of God. It was in Israel, in 1974. The Jerusalem II conference was held in Jerusalem. Kathryn Kuhlman was one of the speakers, along with Jamie Buckingham, Pat Robertson, and David du Plessis. David's message on the love of God from John 17 really got to me. I was undone publically, weeping uncontrollably. Most of that week, I was unable to sleep, overwhelmed with waves of love that continued to come powerfully upon me to the point where I wondered if I would live through it. God's love forever changed me.

Thus, He knew what would happen when He asked us to give Him our mornings. For many years, we had been lovers of Jesus, and we had experienced a new revelation of the Father's love with Jack Winter through the '80s as Jack brought teaching and theology, as well as new revelation, that gave me context for my experience in Israel. But now it was different. God was inviting us into a whole new level of intimacy with Him. We desired to see His presence and power in our ministry, and He was teaching us that it all begins with loving Him. Nothing happens apart from our being deeply, radically in love with Jesus.

Seeking the Anointing

God had asked for our mornings, which was easy enough to do. But the second thing He had asked of us was that we would spend time with anointed people. We knew some; Benny Hinn had been a friend for years. We had actually had him minister in Stratford. We began to seek out others who seemed to be walking in God's power.

This required some sacrifice.

By this time we had joined the Vineyard movement, so of course we were very familiar with John Wimber and what God was doing through him. John's emphasis on Kingdom values with the power of the Holy Spirit was what grounded us when revival hit in '94. We just knew there was more happening on the earth.

Since the mid-1980s, Argentina had been experiencing revival with mass conversions taking place. In 1992, a powerful minister named Claudio Friedzon helped to usher in a new move of God characterized by "being slain in the Spirit, joy and laughter, drunkenness in the Spirit, and praise and adoration of the Lord."[1] Claudio had been influenced by Benny Hinn and Carlos Annacondia, another powerful revivalist. We were drawn to Argentina. Ed Silvoso was taking his annual revival tour. We had to go see what God was up to. It was November of 1992.

There was one problem. We had $500 in our checking account at the time, and no obvious way to get there. We couldn't afford it, but we knew we had to get there somehow. So between our $500 and another $500 from our daughter Lori and our VISA card, we made it.

As Jerry Steingard says in our book *From Here to the Nations,* "We did, indeed, see revival up close."[2] Powerful ministers like Carlos Annacondia, Omar Cabrera, Pablo Deiros, Eduardo Lorenzo, and Hector Gimenez were there, along with Claudio Friedzon himself. It was a powerful time of passion, joy, and freedom.

One night we were invited along with several other pastors on stage to be prayed for by Claudio. Many of the pastors became drunk in the Spirit, falling and rolling and laughing—including Carol. I'm not like Carol though, who kind of goes into orbit spiritually. So after Claudio prayed for me, I just sort of fell over politely. I lay there wondering if I had just taken a "courtesy fall" because I wanted this so badly. I even wondered if he'd pushed me (he hadn't).

I started to get up, rising to one knee. Suddenly, Claudio wheeled around and said to me words that would change my life. "Do you want it?" he shouted. I thought, *Why do you think I spent money I don't have and flew thousands of miles just to be here? Of course I want it.* But all I said was, "Oh, I want it all right."

Claudio said, "Then take it," and he slapped both of my hands. Something happened in me at that moment; it wasn't dramatic like Carol experienced. But something in my heart clicked in a way it hadn't before—*take it.* Be proactive. Up until this point

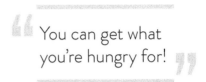

" You can get what you're hungry for! "

I thought that a fresh download of the Holy Spirit would be something that I would be totally passive about as it happened to me; but in that moment, I understood. We needed to pursue it and actively take hold of it by faith.

You see, what we wanted—God's power, encounter, healing—was revival. And when Claudio told me to take it, I understood that revival was mine to take. So I did. I took it. In that moment, I knew something had changed.

Hungry for Revival

Hunger has a target. What are you hungry *for?* God taught us that night through Claudio Freidzon that you can get what you're hungry for. Are you hungry for revival? What are you doing to get it?

In fact, it was being proactive and partnering with God that led to where we are today. We heard about this young pastor named Randy Clark in St. Louis, Missouri. I knew Randy casually as we were in the same region with the Vineyard Movement. As a Baptist pastor, Randy had been quite skeptical about all this "Holy Spirit stuff," but John Wimber and the

Vineyard had changed all that. Now he was hungry for more and desperate for a personal breakthrough. At the urging of a friend, he had attended a Rodney Howard-Browne meeting in Tulsa, Oklahoma. Rodney prayed for Randy, and everything changed. When Randy preached the Sunday after he got home from Oklahoma, he prayed for people—and down they went. No one at his church had ever seen anything quite like that. In the second service that morning, it happened again.

The Holy Spirit began to move powerfully in Randy's meetings, and we heard about it from a mutual friend right after returning from Argentina. Because of the impact of Argentina, we were planning to have monthly healing meetings, and true to our commitment to be around those moving in the anointing, we invited Randy to speak at a short series of those meetings we were planning for January 1994.

> " We pursued God's presence first and foremost, and then we pursued those who were already seeing what we longed to see. "

You know what happened next.

You see, God had spoken a word to us. He had stirred up a powerful hunger to see more of Him, more of His power, more of His healing, and more of His love. But instead of waiting passively for something to fall out of the sky, we pursued the more. We pursued God's presence first and foremost, and then we pursued those who were already seeing what we longed to see. We went after it—and we got it.

God Rewards Our Hunger

The Lord rewards our hunger for Him. He stirs it up, and He won't leave it unsatisfied. When we pursue His presence, He is delighted to be with us. Several years later, I (Carol) bought myself a timer and set it to go off every ten minutes. When my timer goes off, I stop whatever I'm doing and connect with God. I just stop and worship, wherever I am, no matter what is happening around me. I constantly stir up my love for Him, my passion for Him, my hunger for Him. And He always, always responds with love and passion for me.

Twenty-plus years later, we are still as hungry for God's presence as we were then. No—in fact, we're even hungrier for Him today. How does that happen? How have we sustained this hunger for more than twenty years?

When the Holy Spirit fell in 1994, the "Toronto Blessing," as it came to be known, was characterized by several different manifestations. Laughing, shaking, crying, falling down, speaking in tongues—these were things that would happen when the Holy Spirit touched people. There were reports of a gentleman roaring like a lion. Others had visions, and many were so overcome under the power that they couldn't get up off the floor.

He Satisfies Our Soul

Psalm 107:9 says, *"For He satisfies the longing soul, and fills the hungry soul with goodness."* What does God satisfy us with? How does He fill our hungry souls? First with His presence, and then with the fruit of the Holy Spirit. The manifestations can be fun, and it's certainly expected that when the God of the universe shows up in power some things might happen. But the manifestations themselves are not what has sustained and satisfied us for all these years.

Galatians 5:22-23 lists the "fruit" of the Spirit—love, joy, peace, longsuffering, kindness, goodness, faithfulness, gentleness, and self-control. Fruit is what grows on healthy plants that receive the nourishment they need. When we abide in God's presence, as we have learned to do, God provides His fruit in our lives. It's a deep, love-based hunger for more of Him and more of what the Holy Spirit wants to do. Because we have so deeply fallen in love, we have intentionally stayed connected to God's presence through things such as worship and soaking, and the fruit is still coming.

> " The Lord rewards our hunger for Him. He stirs it up, and He won't leave it unsatisfied. "

The Heart of the Father

Many people who came through our doors after 1994 are still walking with the Lord in power today. So many of our critics accused us of "emotionalism"—but if it was just emotionalism, why are so many people still free today? How were so many lives so radically changed?

Many revivals have been characterized by the manifestations of the Holy Spirit. There's nothing wrong with that; sometimes it's how we know God is at work in someone's life. But the core message of what God poured out on all those who came to and were blessed by what happened in Toronto was about the heart of Father God for His children.

Revival isn't about how many people can shake and laugh and fall down. It's not about how much we cry. It's not about how loud our worship is, or how many meetings we have a week. We had no clever advertising. There was no Internet then, nor really any cell phones. We had a fax machine, but the revival spread and people came because real change was happening in friends' lives. People became walking, breathing, living proof that God is real, not just a theory or a tradition.

True revival reveals the heart of the Father for His children. This is what people are hungry for—to know who their heavenly Father is and to know who they are as His children. So many people's hearts and minds were healed as they were touched by God during our meetings, and their testimonies kept a steady stream of hungry people coming, night after night. You see, people want God—and God wants people. It's really just as simple as that.

> Revival isn't about how many people can shake and laugh and fall down. People became walking, breathing, living proof that God is real, not just a theory or a tradition.

What is God saying to you? How hungry are you for Him? Do you have to have more of Him? Ask Him what that looks like for you. The beautiful thing about a heavenly Father like ours is He knows you intimately, and He knows just what you need to stir up the hunger. And even more beautifully, He will satisfy you with good things.

ACTIVATE

Are you hungry for more of God? Take a few minutes right now and focus on Him. Invite Him to come, right now. Pray, "God, would You stir up a hunger in me to see You move mightily, in me and through me? Lord, I don't want anyone or anything but You!"

NOTES

1. Jerry Steingard and John Arnott, *From Here to the Nations* (Toronto, Canada: Catch the Fire Books, 2014), 60.

2. Ibid., 61.

Chapter 3

The More

ONE NIGHT IN OCTOBER OF 1994, MONTHS AFTER THE REVIVAL WAS in full swing, a young man named David Ruis was leading worship at our very first Catch the Fire conference. During the worship service, David was overcome by the presence of the Holy Spirit. He had to stop playing the keyboard because his arms had begun to shake uncontrollably. After trying to control that movement for a few minutes and failing miserably, David surrendered to the Holy Spirit's prompting and began to prophesy.

This is what he declared:

> I am here. I am here. I am here. Am I not He who sits in the heavens and laughs at the plans of men? Has it not already been established from time of old that My King would be established on His holy mountain? I say to you, you thought My movement has begun. I tell you, it has yet to begin. You have seen

nothing, you have seen nothing, you have seen nothing yet. This is just a preparation. You thought the seed is going out amongst the nations of the earth; I tell you that hasn't even begun. I'm just growing up a plant. My rains are coming to grow up a plant that will grow and grow and grow and then come to the place of seed. You thought you felt wind; it has been nothing. My wind shames the greatest hurricanes. My wind shames the greatest tornados. My rain and My wind wreak greater, greater, greater havoc and destruction on the realm of the enemy than any natural thing you have seen. And My wind will blow on this plant and the seeds will go forth to the nations of the earth and bring forth the greatest harvest written page or aural tongue has ever declared in the nations. Give Me glory.

"You haven't seen anything yet," God said. How could that be true? We had seen so much poured out in the months since January; how was it that God was now saying there was *more*?

More, Lord

John Wimber used to pray, "More, Lord." Now here was a guy who was seeing miracles—powerful healing miracles. Here was a guy who regularly experienced the power and presence of God, and yet he was praying for more. After everything we've seen, why would we pray for more?

Some would say that Jesus's work on the cross is finished, complete (it is). Some others might say that the Spirit has been completely poured out on all flesh (He has). So what more is there to be had?

If the Holy Spirit coming upon us is good, then more of the Holy Spirit coming upon us is even better. When I am hungry for food, I eat. But then guess what? In a few hours, I'm going to be hungry again. I'm going to need to have more food. If we are truly hungry for God, then being in His presence only makes us hungry for more. I could never be satisfied with having one meal and never eating again. How could I ever be satisfied with having just one encounter with God?

> If the Holy Spirit coming upon us is good, then more of the Holy Spirit coming upon us is even better.

Read the book of Acts. It seems that although in Acts 2 God poured out His Spirit on all those in the Upper Room (and boy, did He—the townspeople thought they were drunk at nine in the morning), His disciples continually sought more. After being filled once, they pursued being filled again and again and again.

Isaiah 6 describes the Temple:

> *In the year that King Uzziah died, I saw the Lord sitting on a throne, high and lifted up, and the train of His robe **filled** the temple. Above it stood seraphim; each one had six wings: with two he covered his face, with two he covered his feet, and with two he flew. And one cried to another and said: "Holy,*

holy, holy is the Lord of hosts; the whole earth is
full *of His glory!"* (Isaiah 6:1-3)

This passage describes the glory of the Lord. Do you think that's something that can be contained? Measured? Does it ever run out? This picture in Hebrew describes the Lord coming into the Temple—He comes in, and keeps on coming. There is no beginning and no end to Him and His glory. God is infinite. We can never reach the end of Him.

So is there more we can see? More we can access? Yes. There is *more*.

Activate the More

What does *more* look like now? How do we live in an expectation of more every day? It's fine to talk about God's glory, but what does that mean for us? How do we activate the *more*?

This idea of "more" clicked for me (John) one day when I was listening to Francis MacNutt talk about healing. He said

> How could I ever be satisfied with having just one encounter with God?

that if you pray quickly, you will see some results, but if you pray and continue soaking that person in prayer for an hour or so, they're much more likely to come right through with total healing. So we took that thought and applied it to whatever the Holy Spirit wanted to do across the board. If a little soaking is good, then a lot must be better.

Carol is the champion soaker. She will stay with people for hours. I don't know how she does it. Someone has gone down under the power of the Spirit; testimonies go on, the offering has been taken, the sermon is happening—on and on. She will stay right there on the floor beside them all the way through.

And I (Carol) talk to them. Some people want to get up too quickly. Of course God can work quickly, and He often does. But so many times, people get embarrassed or self-conscious and they want to get up before God is done with them. I tell them, "No, you're not getting up. More, Lord. Fire on you." I stay with them; it comforts them, I think. They stay down, and I ask the Holy Spirit to turn up the power on them, give them more—and He does. It's like turning a dial, and you can see it happening; they might start shaking or laughing. I can feel it too.

During the Encounter

But the most powerful part comes when you ask them what God did during that time. The changes can be massive. So many people report seeing God, feeling His love like they never have before, hearing incredible words He speaks to them—the testimonies are awesome. People have reported being healed of physical diseases and being set free from demonic oppression, just right there on the floor. It's life-changing.

You see, it's important to remember that we serve a very good Father who has given us the gift of the Holy Spirit. Jesus said, "*If you then, being evil, know how to give good gifts to your children, how much more will your heavenly Father give the Holy Spirit to those who ask Him!"* (Luke 11:13). Our Father always wants to give us more.

Stewarding the More

One more way to look at this principle of *more* can be found by looking at the way the Kingdom of Heaven works. In what we would call the Parable of the Talents, Matthew 25:15, Jesus tells the story of three men given money by their overseer. The first two men took their "talents," 80 pounds of silver, and invested them, used them wisely—and made more money. The third man hid his talent in the ground; when the master came looking for it, he said that he knew the master to be a hard man, so he had not invested the money. He was afraid to take a risk and buried the money—so what he had was taken away and given to the first man.

Although this parable seems to be directly about money, other Kingdom principles would apply too. It's a matter of stewardship; what do we do with what He has given us? There's a certain amount of testing and proving with God, where He gives you a little and watches to see how you do. When He sees that you are faithful with what He gives you, He knows He can trust you with more. It is the little-much principle. For us, we believe that we are stewarding the presence and power of the Holy Spirit in the way God has told us to steward it. We believe we have been faithful with it. So like Jesus said to one of the first men in the parable, *"Well done, good and faithful servant; you have been faithful over a few things, I will make you ruler over many things. Enter into the joy of your lord"* (Matt. 25:23).

More.

And look—not only do we get more of the thing we steward well, but we get God's love, joy, and peace. How extravagant is He?

Greater Works

In John chapter 14, Jesus says, *"Most assuredly, I say to you, he who believes in Me, the works that I do he will do also; and greater works than these he will do, because I go to My Father"* (John 14:12). Jesus healed every sick person He came into contact with. He raised the dead. He cast the most stubborn demons out. People He touched left His presence more healed, more whole, and with more of His Kingdom in them. While we've seen plenty of healing and deliverance and many other miracles, we are not yet seeing a 100 percent success rate.

> God hasn't shown us how much of Heaven we can have now, but He did say the Kingdom of Heaven is "at hand." That means we can access Heaven—right now.

Are you? But increasingly, it is getting better and better.

On this side of Heaven there is only so much healing and breakthrough we will see; that is true. But how much can we see? How much healing can we see? How many dead people brought back to life? How many captives set free? God hasn't shown us how much of Heaven we can have now, but He did say the Kingdom of Heaven is "at hand." That means we can access Heaven—right now.

We want to see more people healed. We want to see more captives set free. We want to see more dead people raised to life again. We realize that a supernatural life of signs and wonders and miracles is absolutely normal. Read Christian history and you'll find that from the time of Jesus and the apostles through the foundation of the early church and throughout the history of the church, miracles followed. We want those things—and so much more.

There is so much more of God to be had. He is unsearchable, unfathomable, His ways are so much higher than ours; and yet He asks us to search anyway. He delights in our ever-increasing hunger for more of Him.

A Love Affair

How do we cultivate the more? How do we access it? Ignite it?

There are a few ways to step into the abundance of Heaven, but it all begins with a love affair. Being in love with someone creates a desire to be with them more; getting to know the other person's character and strength and wisdom only makes you want to be around them more and more and more. Falling in love with God is no different. The more we know who God is, the more we get to know His character and His personality, the more we fall in love with

> The more we are with Him, the more of Him we will experience.

Him. And the more we fall in love with Him, the more we want to be with Him. And the more we are with Him, the more of Him we will experience.

One of our favorite ways to be in the Lord's presence is through worship. It doesn't matter if you have music or not; you can worship the Lord simply because He is worthy of it. He is worthy of our praises, always. But good worship music is a helpful tool when we want to worship God. And it's important to worship Him in private, when you're alone in your house, as well as on Sunday morning with your church family.

Another way to cultivate God's presence in our lives is by soaking. We'll talk more about that later in this book, but soaking is simply intentionally getting into God's presence and staying there—with no agenda. Just there to be with Him. John and I have been married since 1979, and I still just enjoy being in the room with him. It's even more special with Jesus.

I lie down, and get as still as I can. Then I simply ask Him to come. He always does. Sometimes He talks to me and shows me things. Other times, we just enjoy each other's presence. I find if I'm soaking regularly, I'm very tuned in to His presence at other times. I find it much easier to see what the Holy Spirit is doing in a meeting when I've spent an intimate, rich time in His presence. In other words, I spend time just getting to know who He is so that I recognize Him when He shows up.

John loves to read the Scriptures. He is a great wonderer, always asking "why." His mom used to threaten to write "John-ny's *Why* Book." I'm more a "tell me what to do and I'll do it" girl; I was raised to not ask questions. But John loves to dig into the Bible and find God there. He loves mystery.

Very often when we're reading the Bible together, John will read just a verse or two to me, and we'll wonder about it. Question it. Talk about it. John likes to look up the words in Hebrew or Greek and find out what they meant in those languages. Sometimes he'll come across something we're not seeing today, and he'll ask God about it. Those things will often spark something new—we see it in Scripture, we ask God about it, and then *boom!* We start to see those things happening.

Spend time reading the book of Acts. It's called the "Acts of the Apostles" for a reason—we are to read about what they did and then do those things too. We have the very same Holy Spirit they had, and we are called to do the very same things they did. Here are some examples to read:

- Peter and John heals a lame man (Acts 3:1-11)
- Apostles perform many wonders (Acts 5:12-16)
- Peter and John impart the Holy Spirit (Acts 8:14-17)
- Peter heals Aeneas of paralysis (Acts 9:32-35)
- Peter raises Tabitha to life (Acts 9:36-41)
- Peter delivered out of prison by an angel (Acts 12:7-17)
- Paul heals a crippled man (Acts 14:8-10)
- Paul casts out a spirit of divination (Acts 16:16-18)
- Paul and Silas's prison doors opened by an earthquake (Acts 16:25-26)

- Paul baptizes the Ephesians in the Holy Spirit (Acts 19:1-6)

- Paul heals multitudes (Acts 19:11-12)

- Paul restores Eutychus to life (Acts 20:9-12)

- Paul shakes off a deadly viper (Acts 28:3-6)

- Paul heals the father of Publius and others (Acts 28:7-9)

Reading these stories always extends my faith. Jesus said we would do the miraculous works that He did, and even greater things than He did. The apostles did, and you and I can too.

Give God your time. We've shared how God asked us for our mornings. What does that look like for you? Don't try to figure it out on your own. Ask the Holy Spirit to show you. He knows your schedule and your priorities. Take a half an hour and spend it with Him. But the sneaky thing is, you see, you give Him half an hour and it's so good that you just stay where you are.

> Jesus said we would do the miraculous works that He did, and even greater things than He did. The apostles did, and you and I can too.

The Sacrifice

Asking for more will require sacrifice. It may require you to give up time, or sleep, or other activities. It may require you to lay down your dignity. Having the Holy Spirit come on you more and more may look a little—well, a little peculiar. A little strange. You may find yourself laughing or crying or shaking, and you may even fall down.

God may ask you to pray for people—in public. Many of our people, after spending quality time on the carpet in our sanctuary, say God has asked them to pray for people at the market or the coffee shop or the restaurant. Some have prayed for healing or deliverance, right there at the dinner table. Part of stewarding what God has poured out is this—will we do what He asks us to do with it? Will we sacrifice our reputation in man's eyes in order to see our mission fulfilled? Many people in the restaurants and hotels surrounding our church have gotten healed and been touched by God because people came, got filled up, and went out and poured out the love of God all over the place.

> " He has more healing, more joy, more peace, more love, more everything than we could ever ask or think. The bigger wave is coming. The *more* is on its way. "

Ask God to show you how much He loves the people around you. The whole purpose of God showing up is that people get loved and healed and set free. The *more* that we so desperately want to see is for their benefit.

Surrender

Finally, the main thing that positions us for more is surrender. God, what are *You* doing on the earth? What are *You* doing in my church? What are *You* doing in my family? When we really grasp His thoughts and His plans and we commit to obey what He says, we will see the more of God poured out in our homes, our communities, and around the world.

It's our hunger for God and our hunger to see people healed and set free that positions us to see and receive the more of God. Ask God to help you: "God, I'm hungry. I don't know how to do this. Create in me a hunger for more of You, Lord."

David Ruis prophesied all those years ago that we hadn't seen anything yet. I believe we still haven't. I believe that God has greater things yet to do in Toronto and around the world. He has more miracles than we have ever seen. He has more healing, more joy, more peace, more love, more everything than we could ever ask or think. The bigger wave is coming. The *more* is on its way.

ACTIVATE

God, I surrender to You. I surrender to Your presence, to Your love, to Your Holy Spirit. I want more of You! I believe I haven't seen anything yet! God, right now I choose to lean in to You, to go after more of You—no matter what. I don't know how to do this! Would You create a hunger in me for more and more of You, Lord? I want to be ready!

Chapter 4

The Awareness

STEVE AND SANDRA LONG ARE NOW THE SENIOR LEADERS AT Catch the Fire Toronto, and they have been since 2005 when Carol and I gave the Toronto leadership over to them. Steve recently told me that he remembers things that happened to him when he was around two years old. That's amazing to me. Most of us don't remember things that happened to us when we were that young.

For most people, awareness is something that happens little by little. When you're one or two years old, you're not really aware of all that much. You're usually aware of your mother and father and hopefully aware that you have a calm and peaceful home (babies do pick up on the emotions in the home) as opposed to troubled and chaotic. Then as we grow from two years to about five, we start to be aware of things outside our home environment, like neighbors and friends, the grocery store, church community, and things like that.

When we get to around age five till around age twelve we really become aware of school, our neighborhood, and maybe the town we live in. We start to have books and gadgets and things like that. Hopefully, around this age we become more and more aware of God too. I know I did; my mother was a good Baptist, so she saw to it that my environment was full of things pointing to God. My grandparents also introduced me to the things of God.

Beyond that, we move into the 13 to about 19 or 20 range. This is the stage where we become aware that we are not our parents or an extension of them, but that we have our own thoughts and feelings. We want to have our own lives, our own plans and ambitions. This is also the stage where we become increasingly aware of the opposite sex.

> No one has the complete picture; there is always room to learn and grow.

We begin to think about what we might want to be when we grow up. Do I want to be a police officer? Or a lawyer? Or a teacher, or a nurse? What do you want to be when you grow up?

Worldviews

As we mature and we experience the world around us, there is an ever-increasing awareness of that world. It is physical, it's emotional, and it's spiritual, and this awareness shapes our concept of what's going on, and what "reality" actually is. We call this a "worldview."

I looked up the word *worldview,* and I found a few different definitions:

- A theory of the world used for living in the world.

- A mental model of reality.

- A framework of ideas and attitudes about the world, ourselves, and about life.

- A comprehensive system of beliefs with answers to a wide range of questions.

Actually, there are only two basic worldviews. One, that God or a very intelligent designer created everything and set it in motion. Two, that everything is the result of random chance—which takes a great deal more faith to believe, incidentally.

Our worldview shapes how we see the world around us and how we see ourselves within that world. It also directly shapes how we view others, God, and His Kingdom.

Assuming that we have a biblical worldview, we can often get locked into the way we've always seen things. We develop very strong opinions on what we think is right and what we think is wrong. The way we see the world is automatically right, while the way everyone else sees the world is automatically not right. It would help us all to remember that no one has the complete picture; there is always room to learn and grow.

As I've been praying for more, I've begun asking the Lord for things I'd never thought of before. "God, would You intervene in my worldview? If there is anywhere I'm off course, would You bring me a course correction?"

We all have our own culture and our ideas about what's normal, but they are not necessarily in line with the culture of Heaven. You see, Heaven has a worldview too. And the worldview of Heaven is absolutely right and true and perfect. Your worldview may be one thing, and the worldview of Heaven is another. If they are different, which one do you think should shift? Wouldn't it be better for our worldview to shift and come into line with Heaven and the standard of the Lord Jesus Christ?

What happens is we want Heaven to shift to where we're comfortable. We want Heaven to conform to us, rather than the other way around. But the truth is, that's never going to happen. Heaven will never compromise itself to make us comfortable. So we might as well just say, "Lord, would You intervene in my life and help me to come more and more in sync with the culture of Heaven?"

Most of us need this kind of shift whether we know it or not. Most of us think that we have the right worldview, and everyone just needs to shift to our way of thinking. But no one person has it all right; only Heaven does.

> Intervention from God looks like an encounter with the Holy Spirit, and it brings us into alignment with the things of God.

So how do we make the shift? How do we begin to align more and more with the worldview of Heaven? It's simply through the intervention of God. Intervention from God looks like an encounter with the Holy Spirit, and it brings us into alignment with the things of God. Once God becomes part of your worldview or once your worldview shifts to include more and more of Heaven, you begin to see just how big He is and how kind He is and how smart He is and how powerful He is and how good He is. That heavenly viewpoint allows you to see more and more of what is going on from God's perspective.

Shifting Worldviews

A few years ago, I did a conference in Brussels, Belgium, with a man named Ian McCormack. Ian was a hedonistic surfer originally from New Zealand. He traveled the world surfing and living "the good life."

Once while he was surfing off the coast of Mauritius, he was stung by five box jellyfish. Now if you don't know about box jellyfish, here's what I found about them: "The box jelly-fish's venom is among the most deadly in the world, containing toxins that attack the heart, nervous system, and skin cells."[1] The most toxic animal on earth, and Ian was stung by five of them. To make a long story short, Ian miraculously managed to get an ambulance to the hospital. When he got to the hospital they administered the antidote, but it was too late.

And yet Ian tells a very interesting story. When he was dying in the ambulance, he saw a vision of his mother praying for him. She said, "Son, no matter how far away from God you may be or what you're done wrong. If you call out to God from your heart He will hear you, and He will forgive you."

Well, Ian wasn't a praying kind of person. He didn't even believe in God. But he was so shaken by seeing his mum praying for him on his death bed that he tried to call out to God. The only prayer his mother had taught him as a child was the

Lord's Prayer. And miraculously he was able to pray—asking God to forgive him of all his sins, forgiving others who had sinned against him and surrendering his life to the Lordship of Jesus Christ.

Once he had finished praying, an incredible peace filled his heart which has never left him. Jesus is truly the Prince of Peace!

Upon arriving at the hospital the doctors tried to save his life but it was too late. Ian died in the hospital.

He found himself out of his body. His physical body was dead but he was still alive. He found himself in complete darkness, and wondered if he had actually died or if the hospital had had a power cut and all the lights had been turned off. He couldn't see anything, and when he tried to touch his body, to his shock he couldn't touch anything physical. It was like he was a spiritual being outside of his body.

In the darkness he could hear people screaming at him, telling him that he deserved to be there. When Ian asked where he was a man screamed out that he was in Hell, and to shut up.

As he stood there in the darkness of hades suddenly a shaft of light came down from above. He felt himself lifted up into this incredible light. He then found himself travelling down this tunnel of light, and felt waves of comfort and peace and joy fill his heart.

The next thing he knew, he was in the presence of God. And in that presence was peace that passes all understanding, and more joy, and glory, and serenity than he'd ever thought possible.

He heard a voice within the light ask him if he wished to stay here or return? And that he must see in a new light.

Ian asked him if He was the true light. And he heard Him say, "Ian, God is light and in Him there is no darkness at all!" (1 John 1:5)

Ian realized he was standing in the Presence of Almighty God—and he felt ashamed of all his sins. But waves of pure love came from the Presence of God, and God told him that all his sins had been forgiven when he prayed the Lords Prayer in the ambulance. Ian began to weep like a child, and God's love filled his heart.

Feeling total acceptance and no fear, he stepped into the light and found himself standing before Jesus Christ in His Glorified form. Jesus' hair was as white as snow, and His garments were robes of pure light. And His face shone like the sun in full strength. Purity and holiness filled Ian as he stood before Jesus.

The Lord showed him a new earth and a new heaven directly behind Him. Mountains, fields, flowers, a crystal clear river, and no more death, no more tears or war. Paradise...like a garden of Eden.

Jesus asked Ian, "Do you wish to stay here or do you wish to return?"

Of course Ian said, "Why would I want to go back there? Hell on earth! This is amazing. No, I want to stay here. No one loves me anyway."

But then Ian remembered his mother, who had appeared to him as he was dying. He thought, "She will think I died and went to hell." He changed his mind. "No, I need to go back and tell her that I gave my life to You in the last second of my existence. I need to tell her everything she believes is true. There is a risen saviour...there is a real hell and an amazing Heaven!"

Jesus then showed him his dad and his brother and sister, and tens of thousands of people. Jesus told him that he wanted him to tell everyone what he had seen, as many people would no longer come to church or believe in Him.

Ian chose to come back, particularly for his mother. He thought going back to earth would look like retracing his steps back through the beam of light, back through the blackness, and then finally into his hospital bed. But that's not what happened.

That's not what happened at all.

Jesus said, "Ian tilt your head, open your eyes and see."

He was instantly back in his body—in the hospital morgue.

A doctor was standing over him with a scalpel in his hand, holding his foot. When Ian's eyes opened the doctor was terrified, as Ian had been dead for fifteen to twenty minutes.

Ian heard the Lord say, "Ian, I've given your life back to you."

God began to heal his physical body, and enabled him to walk out of the hospital the next day.

You can just imagine how the doctor responded.

Over thirty years later, Ian still tears up when he talks about this time. Experiencing Heaven and all its beauty and peacefulness and the overwhelming love of God drastically shifted Ian's worldview, and he has never been the same. He now pastors in London, England, and if you talk to him today, he'll tell you that he has absolutely zero fear of death—and an all-consuming passion for life.

What happened to Ian was dramatic, there's no doubt. He had probably heard the Gospel many times in his life, and clearly his mother was a prayer warrior. But nothing changed his perspective until he had this experience with the Holy Spirit. His worldview, rather suddenly and dramatically, came into alignment with Heaven.

Fear of the Encounter

The Holy Spirit coming like this, the Kingdom breaking in on you, tends to throw off constraints you may have had and prepares and empowers you to really begin to sail and to soar in the anointing. But as we've learned, people definitely have constraints where the Holy Spirit is concerned. Many people fear the encounter. They fear the experience. What causes this fear?

One very common fear regarding a Holy Spirit experience is the fear of man, the fear of what others think. Here's Ruth again with her story of how God changed her worldview.

> When my husband and I started the Central (CTF) Campus again, we had a lot of people in our church who didn't love Holy Spirit. How strange is that? I mean, why do you attend a Catch the Fire church if you don't love Holy Spirit?
>
> These people were very opposed to what we were doing, and they would get really angry. If we went over our time by even one minute, they would complain. After every sermon, they had something to say. I just had this fear of man, and I started planning my sermons around thoughts like this: "They probably

won't argue with this, so I can say this. But they might say that, so I won't say that." So much fear.

One Sunday at the end of service, God showed up—on me. He knocked me flat to the ground—in front of those people who were so angry and judging us.

Well, I was on the ground for a good 45 minutes, screaming at the top of my lungs because I thought I was being barbecued. I mean, I was being electrified. My hands were shooting out and my legs were shooting out; I had bruises on my knees afterward from them slamming on the floor like that. There was a puddle of drool under my face, and I was shrieking out notes I know I can't hit. I couldn't do anything.

And I thought, "This is so unattractive." People were wondering where the pastor went; "That would be her, the drooling one on the ground."

I was so embarrassed. I was so aware of the thick presence of the Lord; I just kept thinking, "He might kill me. This is so intense." At the same time, I was aware of those people.

In the midst of this, God said to me, "Me? Or them? Me, or them?" He was asking me to choose. I answered, "You, God. Obviously, You, God." And these waves of His presence kept coming and subsiding and coming and subsiding. "Me? Or them?"

When I got up off that floor, the fear of man was gone. Since then, Holy Spirit's been showing up and doing all kinds of things. It's so wonderful.

It's true that when you're on the floor under the power, other people might feel you are making a spectacle of yourself. And that might bring shame or fear of disapproval on you. The critics ask things like, "Whatever happened to 'decently and in order'?"

We met our now-friend Brian Houston in Orangeville a few years ago at a church dedication. Brian is a popular singer songwriter and worship leader in Ireland.

At this dedication, there were some old friends there who were touched by this revival years ago but weren't particularly open to receiving the anointing of the Holy Spirit anymore. Well, Carol got a little playful, as she does. "Hi there. More, Lord," she would say. And they answered, "Oh, we don't do that anymore," clearly uncomfortable with what was happening.

As Carol was returning to her seat, she gently placed a finger on Brian who was sitting next to her. It felt like the jab of a spear point to Brian and as she sat down she again stretched out a finger to pray for him and again he felt the sharp stab in his shoulder, even though she touched him very lightly. Sensing the Lord was doing something powerful, Carol started praying for him more earnestly. If you've ever had Carol pray for you, you'll know what that's like—the "finger of God" vibe she has.

The heavy weight of God's presence descended on Brian and he started to slide off his chair. His wife, Pauline, was in the row behind him, wondering what in the world was going on. "What is she doing to him?" Next thing you know, he was on the floor. And although not physically touched by anyone, Pauline too slumped like jelly beside her husband.

After the meeting was over, Carol and I decided we wanted Brian and Pauline to really get blessed. So we prayed over them, "Let Your fire come on the two of them, Lord." And they just got electrocuted in the anointing. They were barely able to exit the building.

I realized later that this was embarrassing for them, being out of control in front of their friends. They had never experienced the power of God in such a dramatic and profound way.

About five weeks later, as God would have it, we were in Chicago with Ian Carroll—and so was Brian. Turns out he knew Ian from back in Ireland. When Brian saw us, he thought, "Oh no, they're gonna pick on me again."

Sure enough, I called him up to the platform to give a testimony about what had happened to him in Orangeville. In spite of his misgivings, he came and joined us and I interviewed him.

> The Lord spoke to him. "Oh, you hate this. So let Me get this straight. You like it when you're on stage seeking the spot light, but you don't like it when I decide to lavish my attention all over you?"

I said, "So Brian, what happened to you when the power and the love of the Holy Spirit came on you?" Brian was clearly lost for words but from that moment on and over the next three days of the conference, he was impacted repeatedly, spending most of the time face down on the carpet, the Lord drenching him in His presence again and again.

Brian told me later that on the inside, he was thinking, "God, I can't stand this. These people have singled me out. They're making a public example of me, humiliating me, and I hate it."

Immediately the Lord spoke to him. "Oh, you hate this. So let Me get this straight. You like it when you're on stage seeking the spot light, but you don't like it when I decide to lavish my attention all over you? Son tell me, when did being cool become more important than being mine?" The sword of the Lord went straight into his heart just then. Brian surrendered to what the Lord wanted to do with him and began profoundly repenting, telling the Lord just how sorry he was—and proceeded to get absolutely blasted on the stage. God wrapped His hands around Brian's heart and sovereignly revealed His incredible love and affection for His beloved. When Brian was able to stand again, he was a changed man. Anger, unforgiveness and deep wounds from his past were bathed in the healing balm of his Heavenly Father's touch. That evening in Chicago became a defining moment for Brian in his walk with the Lord.

Not long after this, we invited him to attend a school of leadership in Sheffield, England, with us, and the deep healing and release he experienced profoundly revolutionized his life.

You see, when the Holy Spirit comes, He wants to take over. He doesn't just want to come on you a little bit; He wants all of you. What happened to Brian's worldview was that it shifted to being God-centered. He lost all interest in pursuing his ambitions and received instead a passion for pouring out his gifts for the body of Christ and the lost.

For most of us, the way we view the world is centered on ourselves. Our jobs are about us, our ministry is about us, and our whole lives are centered on us. And then the Holy Spirit invades that picture, we are suddenly jolted from our "me-centered" perspective to coming into alignment with God's view of things.

The Word and the Spirit

I've spent lots of time wondering how this happens. I believe it's a two-fold process—by reading and consuming the Word of God and by the power of the Holy Spirit. In Matthew 4:4, Jesus says, *"It is written, 'Man shall not live by bread alone, but by every word that proceeds from the mouth of God.'"* What an amazing thought, that we need God's Word to live. Luke 16:17 takes that thought a little further: *"And it is easier for heaven and earth to pass away than for one tittle of the law to fail."* In other words, the Word of God is something we can totally rely on, and it is impossible that even one little letter of it will fail.

But it's not just the Word itself. The Pharisees knew each jot and tittle of the law, and yet they were missing something, weren't they? Second Timothy 3:16 says, *"All Scripture is given by inspiration of God."* Other translations say "God-breathed." To properly read and apply the Scriptures in our lives, we still need the breath and inspiration of God.

And where does the breath and inspiration of God come from? It comes from the Holy Spirit. The Scriptures are alive because He, the Holy Spirit, is the author of them. He used 40 or so human beings to write it all out, but He is the author. And when He comes and breathes on them, they come to life.

As we move toward this next wave of revival, let's fall in love with God's Word again. Let's invite His Holy Spirit to breathe on the Scriptures in a fresh way.

No Toxic Levels

The Holy Spirit is so good for you. You can't get too much of Him. Our friend Melinda Fish from Pittsburgh, Pennsylvania, and said it so well a few years ago when she said, "There are no toxic levels of the Holy Spirit." When you have an encounter with Him, you'll never be the same

 The Holy Spirit is so good for you. You can't get too much of Him.

again. So don't be satisfied with just a little bit, with a half-measure of Him. And don't be satisfied with what happened 20 years ago. This constantly being filled is a daily, refreshing encounter with the Holy Spirit.

That being said, it's important to look back on those moments when our entire paradigm shifted and our lives changed forever. These moments serve as milestones, where we can look back and see what God has done in our lives.

Wait for Me in Jerusalem

As I mentioned earlier, I went to a conference in Jerusalem in 1974. I'd never been to Israel before, and it was a big deal for me. I thought, *I'm gonna get ready. I'm going to the Holy Land.* I went on a three-week water fast. I wanted to be ready to meet God in Jerusalem. But my worldview at the time was that God was only after the "truth," and truth as I defined it was about right doctrine. I knew all about the "love of God," or at least I thought I did, but it was really just one more doctrine I had "right."

When I got to the conference, my hero Kathryn Kuhlman was there along with Jamie Buckingham, Pat Robertson, and other heroes of the faith. But the one who really got to me was David du Plessis. David was a South African revivalist, known as "Mr. Pentecost." When he got up to preach, he began to talk about the love of God. Up on the platform with him were all these clergy in their black robes and such—Catholic priests, Anglicans, Presbyterians, Methodists, even a few Pentecostals in their suits.

I sat there watching and listening to all this in judgment, thinking, *What are they all doing up there on the platform? They're probably not even saved.* David began preaching from John 17 about the love of the Father, and the Lord said to me, "Why can't you love people who see things differently than you?" He kept hammering that home, over and over. Every time He did, it felt like an arrow went right into my heart.

He shot my heart full of arrows, to the point where I lost it publicly. I don't do that often; most people have never seen that in me. But it looked like John crying uncontrollably, unable to stop weeping. I could not get it together. It broke my heart to realize that the love of God wasn't just one more thing; it was *the* thing. And I had missed it.

That night in the hotel, my roommate fell asleep well before I did. I lay there, reflecting on the day. All of a sudden, this presence began to come on me like a wave, nice and gentle at first. It was so sweet. Then it would come on again, stronger and stronger and stronger. That happened every night for a week. I felt like I got about five hours of sleep that week...and I can remember saying to Him one time, "God, if one more wave comes on me like that, I'm not gonna live through it."

But I did live through it, and that experience with the Holy Spirit changed my worldview forever. I finally got the revelation that God is love. I still didn't have the theology for it; that didn't come until about ten years later when we had a dear man named Jack Winter come to our new little church in Stratford, Ontario, and begin to teach us about the Father's love.

> "God, if one more wave comes on me like that, I'm not gonna live through it."

Those two things together, the experience and the biblical theology, came together to form a new worldview. If I have any regrets in life, it's that it took me about 45 years to really get it about the love of God.

Rooted and Grounded

For this reason I bow my knees to the Father of our Lord Jesus Christ, from whom the whole family in heaven and earth is named, that He would grant you, according to the riches of His glory, to be strengthened with might through His Spirit in the inner man, that Christ may dwell in your hearts through faith; that you, being rooted and grounded in love, may be able to comprehend with all the saints what is the width and length and depth and height—to know the love of Christ which passes knowledge; that you may be filled with all the fullness of God (Ephesians 3:14-19).

Go ahead and read that again. We are to be "rooted and grounded in love," so that we can really understand how big this deal really is. To know the length and the width and the height and the breadth of the love of God—which by the way surpasses knowledge—so that you can be filled with the fullness of God. Only by knowing the love of God can you be filled.

> Only by knowing the love of God can you be filled.

God's Terms

People sometimes shy away from the power of God because they see the intensity of it. They want it, but they want it on their terms. They want to pick and choose where and when or how it hits them. It's like saying, "I want God, but I want Him on my terms."

> If we truly have experienced more of God and allowed Him to expand our worldviews to align with Heaven, then we'll get to watch as it ends in glory with the return of the Lord Jesus Christ.

No. I want God on His terms. Don't you? Go ahead and let Heaven know right now that you want God on His terms.

You may be reminded of this moment one day when you're on the floor under the power, wondering what the heck is going on. You can't move, you can't get up, and you may feel that embarrassment we talked about earlier.

The question really is, do you want more? I mean, really want it? Because the reality is we need it for what's coming. We are headed into the greatest move of God the world has ever seen; I'm more convinced of it than ever. And it may well come with all kinds of trials and other things, but never mind. If we truly have experienced more of God and allowed Him to expand our worldviews to align with Heaven, then we'll get to watch as it ends in glory with the return of the Lord Jesus Christ.

The Real Miracle

When the Holy Spirit comes upon you, the miracle is not that you fell down or shook or laughed. The miracle is that you lived through it. The Creator of the universe touched you, and you didn't die. *That* is the miracle. He's the One who spoke, "Let there be light," and the sun came out of His mouth. Many suns came out of His mouth. They're all over the universe, aren't they?

Decently and In Order

The question of doing things "decently and in order" kept coming up in the early days. Now, we certainly didn't want indecency and disorder, but you have to ask—whose order are we talking about? His or ours? Look at the day of Pentecost. What did that look like? Fire came and landed on their heads. They spoke

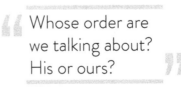

Whose order are we talking about? His or ours?

languages they had never learned. They unlocked the door and poured out into the streets, preaching and prophesying—and prompting Peter to have to say, "We are not drunk." That's somewhat disorderly according to our standards, isn't it?

But out of what seemed to be chaos, 3,000 people got saved that day. So was that decently and in order? I would say yes, according to God's order of things.

His order is different from ours. When man plants trees, he plants them in nice, neat rows, like an orchard. When God plants trees, we get a jungle or a forest, wild and not very "neat." Which order would you prefer? I mean, I like orchards just fine. But there's just something about the wildness of the forest, isn't there?

You see, His ways are not our ways. His thoughts are not our thoughts. In fact, as Heaven is higher than the earth, so is His order higher than ours.

Fruit of Self-control

God's way of planting does produce fruit. Galatians 5 lists out that fruit: "*love, joy, peace, longsuffering, kindness, goodness, faithfulness, gentleness, self-control*" (Gal. 5:22-23). Self-control is a fruit of the Spirit; I think sometimes we forget that. It is for you to control yourself in the context of not giving in to sin. But that fruit was intended for you to control you, never for you to try to control the Holy Spirit.

> Surrender to Him; it's really the best thing you can do.

When He comes, it's best to just surrender; exercise your self-control to give control over to Him. Learn to trust Him.

I'm not talking about surrendering to emotionalism or fanaticism or making anything up. I'm talking about you surrendering to the presence and the power of the Holy Spirit when He comes upon you. Just like Ruth Preston told us, many times it's our own embarrassment that keeps us from surrendering, and God is always asking us, "Me or them?" Who are we really looking to please?

Surrender to Him; it's really the best thing you can do. Surrender when He comes mightily upon you. One of Carol's pet peeves is when people try to get up too soon after being knocked down under the power. It might feel like the anointing is lifting a little, and they begin to get a little self-conscious. "Oh, I'm lying here and all these people are looking at me. I need to crawl away and get up." I've watched Carol literally chase people down because they're not done yet. God's not done yet.

Forget what everybody else thinks. There is nothing more valuable than spending time in the presence of God. It delights His heart when you are out under the power. When you're surrendered in that way, with no agenda on your part, you get strengthened, you get refreshing, you get knowledge, you get revelation—all kinds of really good stuff just by hanging out in His presence. Your worldview gets shifted and expanded to include more and more of Heaven, more and more of God.

As we prepare for the next wave, it's crucial that we prepare our hearts and minds by intentionally going after aligning our worldview with that of Heaven so that when Heaven shows up, we are ready.

ACTIVATE

God, what is my worldview? Am I more concerned with what other people think than what You think? Is my thinking aligned with Heaven? Would You show me where I'm not aligned with You? God, I repent for thinking You are limited! I repent for the ways I've said I don't want You to move. I repent for loving my comfort zone more than You. Would You forgive me? I want to think the way Heaven thinks. I choose You, God! And on Your terms!

NOTE

1. "Box Jellyfish," National Geographic, August 03, 2017, http://www.nationalgeographic.com/animals/invertebrates/group/box-jellyfish/.

Chapter 5

The Suddenly

When the Day of Pentecost had fully come, they were all with one accord in one place. And suddenly there came a sound from heaven, as of a rushing mighty wind, and it filled the whole house where they were sitting. Then there appeared to them divided tongues, as of fire, and one sat upon each of them. And they were all filled with the Holy Spirit and began to speak with other tongues, as the Spirit gave them utterance.

—ACTS 2:1-4

And Suddenly...

How much of Scripture seems to be "and suddenly"? How much of our journey with God seems to be "and suddenly"?

Imagine being one of the original followers of Jesus during His time walking around on the earth. What a roller coaster ride. Three and a half years of the most off-the-charts ministry the world had ever seen. What kind of things did they see?

Imagine walking into a community with maybe a few hundred people in it. In any community, you have sick people, blind people, lame people—people who need healing. And when you walked into those places with Jesus, every single person in that community was healed of everything. Here they were, those people just going along in their lives—blind, deaf, lame, all kinds of sickness. At that time, they didn't know who Jesus was or what He was capable of. Oh, maybe they had heard of Him, but they didn't really know what was possible.

And then suddenly, Jesus came to town. Imagine having been blind since birth or not being able to walk—and then this man comes and touches you or puts mud in your eyes, and then *suddenly* you can see. Limbs grew out where there hadn't been any. Diseases like cancer (although they wouldn't have called it that) just totally healed. Gone. Like they had never existed. Suddenly, all because Jesus showed up.

> Suddenly, there was a sound like a mighty rushing wind—and everything changed.

Now imagine being one of the disciples in the Upper Room. By this time, Jesus had been crucified. Even that seemed to happen suddenly. Imagine the shock of it all—traveling, ministering, healing, and then suddenly the soldiers show up one night and arrest Jesus. Within just a few hours, Jesus is arrested, tried—and murdered. The disciples are in shock; how could this have happened? Everything seemed to have come to a screeching halt.

Even the resurrection had to seem sudden. They saw Him die on a cross, the most horrible way to die anyone could imagine. Nails in His hands and feet, a spear driven into His side—how could anyone not be fully, completely dead?

But then suddenly, three days later, Mary came rushing in to tell them that the grave was empty. Empty. He had done it. He had risen. Then He appeared to the disciples on the road, even cooked them breakfast one day. And all seemed to be on the path to being put right again.

One day, in a room above the street in Jerusalem, the disciples had gathered to celebrate the Feast of Pentecost. Suddenly, there was a sound like a mighty rushing wind—and everything changed.

Everything Changes

On Thursday, January 20, 1994, in the middle of a normal, average church meeting, the Holy Spirit fell—suddenly. Where we had been experiencing church and God and community— and it was good—suddenly now we had this major outpouring of the Holy Spirit. And then suddenly, night after night we had hundreds and then thousands of people coming through our doors. Suddenly, hundreds and thousands of people were getting on airplanes and making hotel reservations and lining up outside our church doors. Suddenly, hundreds and thousands were being touched and healed and changed forever.

Suddenly.

Have you ever experienced a *suddenly* of God? Have you been unexpectedly healed? Or maybe had something like a check come in the mail out of the blue? Or even been going along in your life, not really looking for anything, and then *boom*—God shows up?

All throughout Scripture, God seems to show up quite suddenly. Whether it's an angel appearing or city walls falling down or the long-awaited Messiah suddenly showing up on the scene, God seems to regularly break into our lives, seemingly without warning.

But how sudden is it, really? God often seems to move quickly, and to our experience it can seem very sudden. But if we really look closely we'll see that yes, God moves suddenly—but He always moves right on time. And if we look even more closely, we'll see that it's never as sudden as it seems to us.

The Upper Room

Take the outpouring of the Spirit in the Upper Room. Jesus had actually promised that very thing earlier in the book of Acts:

> *And being assembled together with them, He commanded them not to depart from Jerusalem, but to wait for the Promise of the Father, "which," He said, "you have heard from Me; for John truly baptized with water, but you shall be baptized with the Holy Spirit not many days from now." Therefore, when they had come together, they asked Him, saying, "Lord, will You at this time restore the kingdom to Israel?" And He said to them, "It*

is not for you to know times or seasons which the Father has put in His own authority. But you shall receive power when the Holy Spirit has come upon you; and you shall be witnesses to Me in Jerusalem, and in all Judea and Samaria, and to the end of the earth" (Acts 1:4-8).

And even earlier than that, in John 14:16-18, He said, *"And I will pray the Father, and He will give you another Helper, that He may abide with you forever—the Spirit of truth, whom the world cannot receive, because it neither sees Him nor knows Him; but you know Him, for He dwells with you and will be in you. I will not leave you orphans; I will come to you."* He had already promised that the Holy Spirit would come upon them.

> " The Holy Spirit fell **suddenly**, but yet right on time. "

What happened in Acts 2 was simply a fulfillment of that promise.

They had gathered in the Upper Room to observe the Feast of Pentecost, which was the celebration of God's gift to Moses of the Ten Commandments on Mt. Sinai—fifty days after the Passover Sabbath, which was exactly three days after Jesus, the Lamb of God, had been crucified. The Holy Spirit fell *suddenly*, but yet right on time.

Jesus's Ministry

Even Jesus's ministry while He was here on earth, although it seemed out of the ordinary and very sudden, was the fulfillment of hundreds of promises throughout the Scriptures, throughout what we would call the Old Testament. Isaiah 61 specifically describes who Jesus would be and what He would do. Isaiah 53 had described His death, and then many Scriptures describe what His death would provide for us. Even as far back as Genesis 3, God had a plan in mind. He knew exactly what He would do, and He even knew that it would seem sudden to us.

January 20, 1994

When Carol and I came home from Argentina after being so powerfully ministered to by Claudio Freidzon, we heard that Randy Clark had been similarly touched in a Rodney Howard-Browne meeting, so we invited Randy to come and minister.

He came on a Thursday night, January 20, 1994, and it was kind of a low-key meeting to begin with. There were about 130 of us, not a large crowd, and we worshiped together. Then Randy gave a testimony of how God had brought him through some very dark, depressing times. He told us how the Holy Spirit had come upon him, picked him up, and turned things around for him. Finally, he said to the people, "If you want me to pray for you, just come on and gather around the front."

Sounds pretty harmless, doesn't it? How many meetings have ended just that way? And you go up for prayer, and you have a nice prayer, and maybe you feel something and maybe you don't, and you go home. People began to get up from their seats to come down for prayer—and that's when it happened.

Boom.

Suddenly.

The whole room exploded in laughter and shouting and screaming and carrying on. I don't know how to describe it except to call it what it was—a glorious chaos. There was no managing it; there was only a beautiful letting go.

One of our pastors, Mary Audrey, was teaching in the room next door and heard all the commotion. She heard the uproar and thought, *What on earth are they doing in there?*

She came in the side door and her first thought was, *Where is everybody? I hear all this noise, where are they?* She had imagined a room full of excited people, standing, cheering, shouting and celebrating with great fervency. And then she realized—they're under the chairs. They're between the rows. They're in the aisles. They've just been completely taken over by the Holy Spirit. Her mouth fell open; the next thing she knew, she herself was on the floor, on her face, completely overwhelmed by the Spirit. She was like that for 20 or 30 minutes, and when she got up the second miracle happened—she couldn't talk.

> There are more suddenlies right around the corner that God has been preparing for a long, long time.

That was just the first night. The next night, it happened again. And then again. And again and again and again. And guess what? It's not over. In fact, this is a very young revival, and it's just now getting nicely underway. Oh, there's more to come. There are more suddenlies right around the corner that God has been preparing for a long, long time.

The Secret to the Suddenlies

What's the secret to the suddenlies of God? Are they really what they seem to us, random things that happen when God randomly decides to do them? And if they're not random, how can we see more of them?

There are a couple of secrets to experiencing God's suddenlies. Of course there are things that only God can do—only God could send Jesus. Only God could raise Him from the dead. Only God through Jesus could send the Holy Spirit. And only God could blast a group of 130 people in a room in Toronto, Canada.

But there is a part we can play too. Our love affair with Jesus is not meant to be a master/slave relationship, although He is absolutely our Master. But more than that, God desires our partnership. My friend and president of Catch the Fire World, Duncan Smith, calls it "colleagueship." He says that more than slave, more than son, more than friend, God wants us to be His colleagues, to work alongside Him to see His Kingdom brought to the earth. Preparing for the suddenlies of God is exactly that.

> God wants us to work alongside Him to bring His Kingdom to earth.

The First Secret

The first secret to experiencing the suddenlies of God is to ask. The book of James says we have not because we ask not. So ask. God, would You move in my church? God, would You move in my family? God, I see the way You poured out Your Holy Spirit in the book of Acts. Would You move that way in my city?

The Second Secret

The second secret to seeing God move is to set your expectations. What do you expect God to do? Many people don't see healings, they don't see miracles, and do you know why? Because they don't expect to see those things. They ask for them not really believing that God will do them. But what if we actually expected to see God move? What if we expected Him to do the things we see in Scripture?

Our story was that we had been longing for more. We would cry out to God, saying, "There's got to be a way in the 20th century to see revival. But how can we do that, with our society the way it is now, with everybody working and busy families and all that?" We just didn't see how it could work.

But we had expectations that God wanted it to work. We had experienced Kathryn Kuhlman's ministry. We had experienced Benny Hinn's ministry.

> " If you want to see God move, you have to expect that He will. "

We had experienced Claudio Friedzon and what was happening in Argentina. And of course we were familiar with John Wimber's ministry. We had experienced many powerful touches from God ourselves and had seen thousands touched. So we had an expectation that God would do it again. And we wanted Him to do it through us.

If you want to see God move, you have to expect that He will. He is always up to something; it's up to us to choose to look for it. How do we know what to expect? If you haven't seen a powerful move of God before, just go back to the Scriptures. Part of the reason God gave us the written Word was so that we could have a picture of what He wants to do on the earth. The book of Acts is a great place to start if you want to know what to expect when you ask God to move mightily.

Setting expectations might actually be called building up our faith. Romans 10:17 says that faith comes by hearing. It comes by seeing, too. Once you've seen God open a deaf ear, you can never un-see it. Once you've seen God grow a limb where there wasn't one before, you can't pretend you don't know it's possible. I believe that one of the reasons God asked us to hang around anointed people was so that we could see what He wanted to do through us.

This can be a challenge for some of us, though. Many people are skeptical of a move of God like this. They may not experience it themselves even if they see someone else experience it, and because they are not feeling it they think it's not real. They think it's being faked. In our day, we put a lot of value on our intellect, on how smart we are. We work hard to become great *thinkers*. We get the answers right and call that "faith."

But Jesus called us to a different kind of faith. In Matthew 18:3, Jesus says, *"Assuredly, I say to you, unless you are converted and become as little children, you will by no means enter the kingdom of heaven."* What does He mean? Is He asking us to not be mature? No, what Jesus is actually saying is that child-like faith is maturity. Innocent, simple faith that believes what God says is real and that expects Him to do what He says He will do. That's the mark of a mature believer, not complicated doctrine and fancy arguments.

How do we build faith like that? First of all, we have to repent of thinking we know it all. We have to decide that God is God and we are not, and if He wants to wreck an entire room full of people on a Thursday night in Toronto, He can do that. If He wants to make toes grow out, He can do that. If He wants to make 120 people look like they're drunk at nine in the morning, He can do that.

The Third Secret

Third, we have to repent of the idea that the Holy Spirit is a "gentleman." Now of course, He can be gentle and usually is. It is one of the fruits of the Spirit (see Gal. 5:23). But not always. It was God's power that blinded the apostle Paul and silenced Zachariah the father of John the Baptist. Then of course, there was Ananias and Sapphira. For years, I read the account of Acts 2 with the idea that when the Holy Spirit fell on them, it meant that it was this nice, gentle Spirit that came in like a breeze, and the next thing you know people are speaking in strange languages and acting like they're a bit drunk in the streets.

> We need to set our expectations by what Scripture shows us, not the other way around. We need to repent of determining what God will and won't do based on what we've already experienced or understood.

I don't think that way anymore.

I think it was more like a bomb went off or a hurricane blew through the room. The God of the universe swirled in there, flames of fire were blazing on their heads, and the whole room was overpowered by the invasion. The city was in an uproar; picture how it would look if 120 people were roaming the streets of your city, acting like they were drunk, and obviously uneducated, but miraculously speaking—in native languages of the many visitors—the wonderful works of God. Would it be a nice, calm picture? Or would there be chaos and mayhem?

We need to set our expectations by what Scripture shows us, not the other way around. We need to repent of determining what God will and won't do based on what we've already experienced or understood. None of the people in the Upper Room had ever experienced anything like that, but He did it anyway.

So we need to expect God to show up and expect that He will do things His way. (He's much better at doing ministry than we are anyway. It's better to just let Him have His way.)

The Final Key

The final key to experiencing God's suddenlies is to wait on Him. In Luke 24:49, Jesus tells the disciples to "tarry." Many times we think of waiting as passive, like I'm just going to sit here until God moves on me. And there's a time for that. But I don't think the disciples in the Upper Room were being passive. They knew what He had told them He would do, even if they didn't know what it would look like. And they put themselves in a position to see that happen. They gathered together, expecting. I really think that the day they gathered in the Upper Room was not the first time they had gotten together. They actively chose to put themselves in a position to receive what Jesus said they would receive. They did the part they could do and waited for God to do what only He could do.

We knew what God had said would happen in Toronto. Many prophetic words over many years had set our expectations high. We knew something would happen; we knew God would keep His word. We didn't know what it would look like, but we actively put ourselves in a position to receive whatever He wanted to pour out. When we invited Randy Clark, it was an act of tarrying, of putting ourselves in a place to see God move.

> You don't know when, so why not make room for it to happen all the time? Expect it to happen.

If God has promised you that He will move in your church or in your life, He will. You can count on that. It's not a matter of if, it's a matter of when. You don't know when, so why not make room for it to happen all the time? Expect it to happen.

Ask Him to come. Expect Him to come. And then wait for Him to do what He says. Suddenly.

ACTIVATE

God, I repent of thinking I know what You want to do and how You want to do it! I'm sorry I've put myself in Your place. I know You've made promises to me to show up; I won't tell You how to do that! Lord, would You show me how and when to position myself to see more of You? I choose to not make my experience or lack thereof my standard. I will read Scripture, I will listen to others, and I will go where You are moving. God, move in my life! Move in our nation! Move in our world! Come, Holy Spirit!

Chapter 6

The Visitation

The spiritual beauty of the Father and the Savior
seemed to engross my whole mind; and it was
the instinctive feeling of my heart, "Thou art;
and there is none beside Thee." I never felt such
an entire emptiness of self-love or any regard to
any private, selfish interest of my own. It seemed
to me that I had entirely done with myself. I
felt that the opinions of the world concerning
me were nothing, and that I had no more to
do with any outward interest of my own than
with that of a person whom I never saw. The
glory of God seemed to be all, and in all, and to
swallow up every wish and desire of my heart.
—SARAH EDWARDS, *wife of Jonathan Edwards*[1]

FOR A WHILE, THERE WAS A STATEMENT GOING AROUND THAT SAID,
"We don't want God to merely visit; we want Him to remain."
We don't just want a visitation from God, we want a habitation;

we want Him to stay with us all the time. This can easily be a misunderstanding of a revival culture like the Toronto Blessing. What the media reported and what most people saw were the experiences, the mountaintop highs that people would have when they came.

But what didn't get reported were the love affairs that began there on the carpet in our sanctuary. What didn't get reported were the thousands and thousands of lives transformed from the inside out. What reporters didn't talk about were the generations of families that were now living for God and living in victory where there had only been defeat in the past.

Habitation

Of course we want a habitation. Of course we want the presence of God to remain long after the service has ended. This is our goal. It's all we've ever wanted. It's true that He's not McJesus—He isn't a "drive-thru" Savior we just rush past, get what we want from Him, and get out. That's not who He is at all.

I (Carol) believe that my relationship with Jesus is just one big love affair. And although love affairs take time, love affairs sometimes begin with a big bang. There's a magical moment when your heart opens to the other person, and it's what we might call "falling in love." When that moment happens with Jesus, our hearts open wide and He comes right in. But don't think that it's accidental. Jesus has been pursuing and pursuing and pursuing your heart for a long, long time before that moment happens. There's a reason that so many books have been written about the "divine romance." We are made for it. Our hearts long to be deeply loved and to deeply love.

In Luke 10, Jesus commends Mary for sitting at His feet. I imagine her sitting there, gazing up at Him quite lovingly. She sat as He taught, as others came and went, as Martha hurried around being busy. She lingered in His presence, but there was a moment, a single moment, when she stopped whatever she had been doing and sat down in front of Jesus. In fact, all of the disciples had a moment when they stopped what they were doing and followed Jesus, when their love relationship with Him began.

> Our hearts long to be deeply loved and to deeply love.

Falling in Love

In a revival, that's what happens all the time. People come and encounter God. Their hearts open up to Him, and they fall in love. Those moments of visitation are precious. And as long as I've been a lover of Jesus, I've had many, many moments of visitation when one more time Jesus comes and woos my heart.

Think of a marriage. There's a moment of engagement when the man asks the woman to marry him. That's a pretty big moment. For most people, it can be a very emotional encounter, sometimes with tears and laughter. It's romantic and wonderful.

Then hopefully throughout the marriage, there are other romantic moments as well—the celebration of an anniversary, a birthday, holidays, or even just for no reason at all, just because two people love each other and want to express that love. Those moments are very important to the relationship. Don't we love those times, when our beloved just focuses all their love on us and we feel all lovey and mushy and have stars in our eyes? Of course we do.

Intimacy

Kathryn Kuhlman once said, "God is more real to me than any human being." For a long time, I wondered what she meant by that. People are very real to me. How could God be more real?

Then I realized what she was talking about—she was talking about intimacy. Intimacy can be stated as "into-me-see." I know you, and you know me. I mean, really know each other in a deep, deep way. She was talking about an ongoing, passionate, intimate love relationship between us and God.

Everything flows from our intimacy with God. So what does this look like?

Three Journeys

Our relationship with God can be described in three parts— inward, upward, and outward. In other words, our personal, intimate relationship with God (inward), then our lives as worshipers of Him (upward), then our relationships with others around us (outward). This describes the life of every believer.

Inward Journey

Our inward journey begins with God wanting to save us from sin and judgment but then sanctify us, free us, and heal our hearts. All of us have hurts and wounds that we've carried for a long, long time, many since birth. These wounds are covering up the person God made us to be. They cause us to act in ways that may hurt other people. They keep us from being and experiencing all that God has for us.

This journey is just for you. You see, God the Father knows that we've learned to live like orphans, like children without a Father. He knows that we've decided we can make our own way, do it ourselves, and we don't need anybody else. He also knows that's not true. God is your Father, and He offers you the spirit of adoption by which you get to be called a son or daughter. You get to rest in the presence of a good Dad with everything that He has. He knows you. He knows everything about you. And He really loves you. Isn't that good news?

> He knows everything about you. And He really loves you. Isn't that good news?

Because He really loves you, He wants to heal your heart. He wants to get to all those wounded and hurting places and heal them, restore them, renew them. He doesn't just put Band-Aids on; He makes it all new again.

Early on in our ministry, we were deeply impacted by John and Paula Sandford and their inner healing ministry. We were transformed by John and Paula's message of dealing with and repenting of bitter roots in our hearts so that we can be healed. They taught us that we couldn't just change our behaviors;

we have to always go after what's in our hearts because Jesus wants to heal our hearts. Our behavior can show us where we're hurting, but it's only God who can heal us.

Upward Journey

The second part of the journey is the upward journey, where we learn to live a lifestyle of worship and prayer. God is looking for those who will worship Him in Spirit and in truth. I want to be one of those people. God is worthy of our worship, always, no matter what. In fact, in Heaven right now there's a big worship service happening. Millions are singing to Him right now, just like Revelation says. The four living creatures are constantly saying, "Holy, holy, holy." The twenty-four elders are forever telling Him how worthy He is. And we get to participate, right now.

I (Carol) have always been a worshiper. I love to worship. When Jeremy and Connie Sinnott were our worship leaders, Jeremy always liked the way I worshiped. He would get me on the platform—and turn off my microphone. I'm so grateful for the Scripture that tells us to make a joyful noise unto the Lord. Just wait till I get to Heaven. I've got a voice on order, and you're going to be so sick of hearing me sing. I can't wait to worship Jesus forever.

As important as it is to worship in a church service, it's important to learn to worship Him by yourself, in your own room. It can be easy to sing and dance when there are instruments playing. But where we really learn to be worshipers is in those intimate times with the Lord when we get alone with Him and just worship. We might sing along with worship CDs. Sometimes I like to read the psalms out loud. Sometimes I just like to love on Him and tell Him how wonderful He is. One of the most wonderful things about Him is when I stop and worship Him, He always loves me in return. When I tell Him how wonderful He is and how much I love Him, He returns the love. Although I worship Him just because He's worthy of it, He is so full of love—in fact, He *is* love—that He can't help but love me right back.

Several years ago, as I was learning to fall in love with Jesus, I got a digital timer. I set the timer to go off every ten minutes; when it goes off, I stop what I'm doing and I worship God. I just tell Him how much I love Him. I tell Him how good He is. With our cell phones and other things today, that's very easy to do. Just set an alarm that reminds you to focus on your upward journey and worship God. Worship isn't actually an event or a service or even just a part of our quiet

> " When I tell Him how wonderful He is and how much I love Him, He returns the love. "

time. It's a lifestyle. We should live in such a way that everything we do is worship. Having my timer to remind me taught me how to always focus on Jesus, to always focus on His goodness, to always invite His presence into my life.

Living this way is actually spiritual warfare. You see, our battle isn't so much with the demonic, although demons are very real and we are definitely at war with them. But our battle, especially these days, is for intimacy with God. Closeness with Him. Knowing Him and being known by Him. There are so many things, so many voices, that would pull us away from Him, and it can be a real battle to maintain that love relationship. But if we are truly intimate with God, the devil's power is thwarted in our lives. The more intimate we are with Him, the more secure we are, and the more the lies of the devil just fall off of us.

Just like my relationship with John. There are so many demands on my time and my heart. We have children, we have responsibilities, we pastor people, we travel extensively; all of those things are good things, but they can all chip away at my time with my husband. If I want to have a happy, healthy marriage, I have to fight for my time with him. I have to set aside other things, sometimes very important things, and say no to them so that I can say yes to time with my husband.

It's the same with our relationship with Jesus. We can get so busy doing the good things that we forget the best thing. Jesus told Martha that Mary had chosen the "best" thing; she had chosen to be in His presence above anything else. Worship and soaking are the primary ways we can do that (we'll talk about soaking later in the book). We set aside everything else and just focus on God.

Outward Journey

Finally, our spiritual journey has a third piece—the outward journey. I love what Jesus said in John 7: *"If anyone thirsts, let him come to Me and drink. He who believes in Me, as the Scripture has said, out of his heart will flow rivers of living water"* (John 7:37-38). We drink first, and then we let what we've drunk flow out to those around us. We are meant to be receivers and releasers of the Kingdom of Heaven, right here on earth. But we have to receive, we have to drink, first. That's why we focus first on getting our hearts healed and whole, and then we worship Him.

When we worship, although our hearts and minds are focused on Jesus, we can't help but get filled up at the same time. Anytime I'm in His presence, I get filled up with more and more of Him. He enables us to worship Him and to love Him with all our heart and with all our soul and with all our strength according to the Great Commandment (see Matt. 22:37). And then according to the Great Commission, He sends us out to share the Good News, the Gospel, with a world that desperately needs what we have (see Matt. 28:19-20).

It's so easy to get stuck in the inward and upward journey. Basking in the love of a good Father and having our hearts healed is so good. And worshiping Him for hours and hours is a joy. And He loves when we do that. But it's not just about the inward and the upward; it's about the outward too. It's about going and pouring out what we've been given into the lives of so many others. We have a job to do. The lost are really lost, and hell is real, and we have a very important assignment.

> Just like Jesus pursued us and wooed our hearts, so He is pursuing others and wooing their hearts as well. This isn't the kind of love affair where nobody else gets to share it. This one is for the whole world.

Sometimes, this can be the hardest part of the journey. We must understand that just like we had that moment of visitation with Him, we are to invite others into the same type of moment. Just like Jesus pursued us and wooed our hearts, so He is pursuing others and wooing their hearts as well. This isn't the kind of love affair where nobody else gets to share it. This one is for the whole world.

For the Nations

When the Spirit fell in 1994, we knew that it wasn't just for Toronto, but it was for the nations. David Ruis's song "Let Your glory fall in this room; let it go forth from here to the nations" became our theme song. We knew that our role was to create a place where the Holy Spirit introduced people to the love of the Father and to an intimate relationship with Jesus. This is how it just went on and on and on for 12 years of nightly meetings. Because ordinary people, just like you and me, would come and get filled up and then pour out on others. "Lord, would You use me?" they would ask. They would get filled up and then take it back to their homes at the four corners of the earth.

The Orphans Come Home

The goal of these visitations, like the one we experienced in Toronto and many others, is to provide that moment of experience where hurting and wounded and lost orphans are introduced to their loving heavenly Father. It's where He begins the process of healing their hearts. It's where they learn what worship looks like and that He is worthy of it. It's the beginning—and it's so important. We must understand that the truth is this—the Spirit of God will nurture a deep and meaningful relationship in every believer when they come to know Jesus as their Savior, the Father as their heavenly Abba (Daddy), and the Holy Spirit as their close and faithful friend. He doesn't leave—He inhabits us. We are called to live in such a way that we cultivate and nurture that relationship, that we choose to fall in love with Him more and more every day.

But as we look forward to this bigger wave that's coming, we invite the visitation of God to come in power. We long for an unusual release of His glory and His presence and His power among us. We want the visitations—we want lots of them—that lead to a habitation for everyone who encounters the presence and power and love of God. We want the engagement question that leads to an eternity of love.

> We long for an unusual release of His glory and His presence and His power among us.

What can you do today to cultivate your love affair with God? Consider setting an alarm on your phone that reminds you to turn and worship Jesus for a while. Set aside some time today just to worship Him. Invite Him to come and heal your heart. Then ask God to show you how you can pour out on those around you. Who needs a touch from God? Freely you've received, freely give.

ACTIVATE

Jesus, would You show me the best thing? Would You please show me where I've put things ahead of You? I know I get busy, and I sometimes forget to just sit at Your feet, Jesus. Today I choose to stop my busyness, to still the noises, and sit with You. I want to fall more and more in love with You, Jesus!

NOTE

1. David Francis Bacon, *Memoirs of Eminently Pious Women of Britain and America* (New Haven, CT: Daniel McLeod, 1833).

Chapter 7

The Anointing

The Spirit of the Lord is upon Me, because he has anointed Me....

—LUKE 4:18

I WANT TO CHALLENGE YOU AS YOU READ THIS CHAPTER TO NOT just let it be information. Let the topic of the anointing spread from your head all the way down to your toes. Ask the Holy Spirit to show you exactly what I'm talking about. Pray right now: *"Come, Holy Spirit. Don't let this be just one more chapter in a book. I'm asking for an encounter with You! Anoint me, Holy Spirit!"*

Someone once asked Randy Clark why people fall down. Without missing a beat, he answered, "Because they can't stand up."

The Toronto Blessing has been characterized by lots of people falling down, shaking, laughing, or crying. But what we call the manifestations are only evidence of what's really going on—people are responding to the presence of the Holy Spirit. I asked the Lord once why He likes it when people fall down. What He said to me was, "Because when people fall down, there are generally two issues being addressed—fear and pride. It's not the same when you're sitting down and someone prays for you, or even when you're already kneeling; you still get to hold on to your dignity. But when the Holy Spirit takes you down to the floor, He is addressing both fear and pride in you."

Now, I'm not talking about what we call a "courtesy fall"; you know, where you feel like you have to fall down. Nor am I talking about being pushed over. That's not helpful at all. I'm talking about when the Holy Spirit comes on people with power and moves upon hearts and lives. We call that "the anointing."

Anointing

The word *anointing* actually means to be smeared with oil or ointment. In the Old Testament, new kings would have oil poured on them, symbolic of the Holy Spirit coming upon them to enable the person to function in the office into which God had placed him. This practice was followed for commissioning prophets, priests, and kings. That's what happens when the Holy Spirit comes on us—we are smeared with the oil of His presence. It gets all over us, from our head to our feet, and we are empowered to be kings and priests and prophets on the earth. We have been anointed.

We are talking about a life-giving Spirit. In John 6:63, Jesus says, *"It is the Spirit who gives life; the flesh profits nothing. The words that I speak to you are spirit, and they are life."* This is weighty; He says here that without the Spirit, anything you do is not profitable. In Luke 4, Jesus makes the bold claim, *"The Spirit of the Lord...has anointed Me"* (Luke 4:18). Even Jesus couldn't do ministry without the anointing of the Holy Spirit.

John Piper describes the Holy Spirit this way: "The Holy Spirit is the eternal love that flows between the Father and the Son as they delight in each other."[1] Wow. The eternal love that flows. That's weighty. And it is weighty when the anointing comes upon you; that's why so many people find themselves knocked down. It also explains why so many find such joy (laughter) or they shake and roll on the floor. When the "eternal love" comes upon you, it might make you shake.

> When the Holy Spirit takes you down to the floor, He is addressing both fear and pride in you.

Go Deeper

The deeper we go in the anointing, the less control we might have. Galatians 5:22-23 tells us that there is fruit that comes with the anointing, including love and joy and peace—and self-control. But self-control means God gives you control over you to defeat issues of sin and wrong choices, not to have control over the Holy Spirit. When we say, "Come Holy Spirit," we want Him to come and do whatever He wants to do. To the world, that might look messy or out of control. But when you're under the anointing, you're not out of control; you're gloriously under His control.

There was a time I was in New Zealand, and some of the guys I was with told me that the best fishing in the world is in the rivers there in New Zealand. So I made a point of having a couple of extra days just to check out their claims.

It had just rained like crazy, and so, for whatever reason, we didn't even see a trace of a fish, much less catch one on a hook. But I did go into the river with some hip waders on. When I waded in so the water was just over my feet, I was fine. No problem. Then I went a little further in, about up to my knees, and it was a little more work to stay in place. I didn't want to fall down. I could feel the current of the river, and who knew where it would take me. By the time we waded in up to our waists, I realized we were really no longer in control here.

> But the deeper we go, the more the Holy Spirit can direct us, and before we know it we're gloriously in over our heads in Him.

In Ezekiel 47, the writer describes a river that flows from the Temple of God. The man—who I imagine to be Jesus—measured 1,000 cubits out into the river, and the river was ankle deep. As I found out in New Zealand, ankle deep is no big deal. I'm definitely still in control. But then, another 1,000 cubits farther out and the river was up to his knees. Again, not a big deal, but a little less control. One thousand more cubits, and the water is now up to the man's waist—and he measures out 1,000 more after that, and the writer says the water is too deep; he can't cross the river. If he goes into that river, he will go whichever way the river flows.

The Holy Spirit is like that. When we wade in a little bit, things are still mostly under our control. But the deeper we go, the more the Holy Spirit can direct us, and before we know it we're gloriously in over our heads in Him. At that point, He's in control, and we go where He wants us to go.

There are so many analogies to describe the Holy Spirit— river, fire, wind, rain, oil, and even wine. With each one of these things, the more of it there is, the less control we have over it. When we come under the anointing, the smearing of the Holy Spirit, we get filled to overflowing.

Ministry

There's something more that happens in our hearts as we get immersed in the Holy Spirit. The more of Him we receive, the more of Him we can contain. It's as if the more anointing we get, the more anointing we can carry. This is how the "outward" part of the journey that we talked about in Chapter 5 works—we get so full of the Holy Spirit that it overflows.

This overflow is what we might call "ministry." Probably the greatest revival ever was recorded in the book of Acts. I think what we're about to see might eclipse even that; but nevertheless, that's the greatest revival thus far. The whole Roman world was completely converted to Christianity. Think about that for a minute—how do you take a pagan world that worshiped all the many gods of Greece and Rome, had it all thoroughly entrenched in their culture—including worshiping the emperor mingled with rampant sensuality and all kinds of other crazy things going on—and make a real difference? Imagine going to Caesar and saying, "A couple hundred years from now, your whole empire will turn away from the gods of Greece and Rome and will worship the Jewish God as He is revealed through Messiah Jesus. How do you like that?"

What would Caesar have said? Probably that you were crazy, that it would never happen. He would probably have you executed for suggesting such a thing. But it did happen, because those who had received from the Holy Spirit were ministering out of that river.

The Integrity of the Minister

Without this anointing of the Spirit, we are ministering in the flesh. We certainly don't want to settle for that. Sometimes we are impressed with ministers and leaders who are anointed, but what if the character or integrity of that minister doesn't seem to match the anointing? No one is perfect, of course, and we live with the provision of grace and forgiveness, but don't mistake grace for license and a lack of integrity. It's important that the character of the minister is growing to match the character of the Holy Spirit in whom he or she ministers. For us as ministers, as we seek revival, we need to work on our character. We want to be Christlike in character and anointing.

Ministering under the anointing can be heady stuff. It can be exhilarating. And it is. It's more fun than I've ever had. But sometimes the attention you get from what happens when you minister can go to your head. It can play to your woundedness, your insecurity, and it's easier than you might think to make it about you and how gifted you are rather than God and how it's all about Him. It's easy to fall into a "look at me, watch me" kind of thing. We might call that pride—which can actually stop up the river. It's the flesh, not the Spirit.

But humility—recognizing that without God I can do nothing—is the thing that will keep your spirit open and ready to receive when He pours out. I think that's why God loves to knock us down; it's hard to be prideful when you're laughing and shaking in front of everybody. And if you're not sure what that looks like, just let Carol get her hands on you.

> As we seek revival, we need to work on our character. We want to be Christlike in character and anointing.

As we look forward to the greater wave, we need to stay humble. We need to stay in a place where we're ready to receive, no matter what it looks like—no matter what it may do to our pride. In fact, we should be ready to lay down our pride. Crucify it. We only boast in Jesus.

Honor the Anointing

Another crucial piece of revival is honoring the true anointing of those around us, especially leaders. Honor comes from that place of humility.

In Mark 6:4, Jesus said, *"A prophet is not without honor except in his own country, among his own relatives, and in his own house."* What is the result of not having honor? Watch what happens: *"Now He could do no mighty work there, except that He laid His hands on a few sick people and healed them. And He marveled because of their unbelief"* (Mark 6:5-6). Because they did not honor Him and His anointing, He could do "no mighty work there."

Wow. That's heavy. How often have we been frustrated because it seems God isn't doing mighty works among us? We're not seeing the miracles and healings and dead raising we'd like to see. We're not seeing revival break out the way we really want to. Oh, maybe there are a few little things here and there—some laughter, a few tears, maybe a head cold gets healed. But that deep part of the river doesn't seem to be flowing.

It's possible that someone has dishonored another leader. Maybe that someone is you. I've done it. I've grumbled and complained about my pastors and leaders in the past. But how could this happen to Jesus? How could He be limited in what He could do?

Think about Jesus for a minute. He's Jesus. He's the Son of God. He *is* God. He is always, eternally, filled with the Holy Spirit. And then He became small, the size of the point of a pin, and came into the body of a girl named Mary. Yet of course He was still filled with the Spirit. In Luke 1, Mary goes to visit Elizabeth. In Luke 1:41, it says this: *"And it happened, when Elizabeth heard the greeting of Mary, that the babe leaped in her womb; and Elizabeth was filled with the Holy Spirit."* Jesus was already eternally filled with the Holy Spirit. When Mary, carrying Jesus, came into the room and greeted Elizabeth, the Holy Spirit anointed Elizabeth.

Then Jesus was born. Just like us, He had to learn to walk and talk and how to read and write. He grew up in a little town named Nazareth, probably playing and going to school with other boys His age. They had neighbors who knew Jesus as just one of the boys. Except for the one report when Jesus was about 12, there's nothing written about Him doing any kind of ministry until He was 30 years old. He was a person, living in a town, doing what people do.

Then He heard that His cousin, John, was baptizing out in the River Jordan. So to fulfill all righteousness, He went out to John and said, "I want you to baptize Me." John tried to argue, but Jesus insisted. John baptized Jesus, and the Holy Spirit descended like a dove, and His Father affirmed Him, saying, *"You are My beloved Son; in You I am well pleased"* (Luke 3:22).

It's interesting here what the Father said about Jesus communicates so much more than the dove coming down. He said to Jesus, "I love You—and I also like You." Part of the baptism of the Holy Spirit is an affirmation of the Father to us, that He loves us, but He also likes us. Sometimes we say things about other people like, "Well, I love that person, but I don't really like them." But here's the Father, showing us how to love in the Spirit.

After Jesus was baptized, He went out into the wilderness to be tempted by the devil. Mark's Gospel actually says it was the Spirit who drove Him there (see Mark 1:12), and Jesus obeyed the Spirit. For forty days, He fasted in the wilderness. At the end of the forty days, the devil came and tempted Him with power and with influence. His Sonship was being questioned, challenged, and tested, but Jesus knew who His Father said He was, and He knew what His Father had given Him access to, and He was able to resist the temptation—which positioned Him for the actual power and influence He was supposed to have.

Who Does He Think He Is?

So now we come to Luke 4:14: *"Jesus returned in the power of the Spirit to Galilee."* He returned, full of the Spirit and under the anointing. Here's the story:

> *Then Jesus returned in the power of the Spirit to Galilee, and news of Him went out through all the surrounding region. And He taught in their synagogues, being glorified by all.*
>
> *So He came to Nazareth, where He had been brought up. And as His custom was, He went into the synagogue on the Sabbath day, and stood up to read. And He was handed the book of the prophet Isaiah. And when He had opened the book, He found the place where it was written:*
>
> *"The Spirit of the Lord is upon Me,*
> *Because He has anointed Me*
> *To preach the gospel to the poor;*
> *He has sent Me to heal the brokenhearted,*
> *To proclaim liberty to the captives*
> *And recovery of sight to the blind,*
> *To set at liberty those who are oppressed;*
> *To proclaim the acceptable year of the Lord."*
> *Then He closed the book, and gave it back to the attendant and sat down* (Luke 4:14-20).

He sat down. He read the most Messianic passage from the Old Testament He could have chosen, closed the book, and sat down. The rest of verse 20 says this: *"And the eyes of all who were in the synagogue were fixed on Him."* I'll bet they were.

And I think all eyes were on Him, not just because He read the passage but because of *how* He read it. I think He read it this way, strongly with emphasis!

> *The Spirit of the Lord is upon* **Me**,
> *Because He has anointed* **Me**
> *To preach the gospel to the poor;*
> *He has sent* **Me** *to heal the brokenhearted,*
> *To proclaim liberty to the captives*
> *And recovery of sight to the blind,*
> *To set at liberty those who are oppressed;*
> *To proclaim the acceptable year of the Lord.*

Jesus was being very clear that He was applying this Scripture to Himself. Then He goes even further and says, *"Today this Scripture is fulfilled in your hearing"* (Luke 4:21). Can you imagine? I can picture this crowd of people sitting there with their mouths open. They have heard this Scripture read to them their entire lives, and they know it's about the Messiah. *What did he just say?* Luke reports, *"And they said, 'Is this not Joseph's son?'"* (Luke 4:22).

In other words, they begin to ask, "Who does Jesus think He is? Surely little Jesus from down the road isn't calling Himself the Messiah. That's ridiculous." But Jesus, being Jesus, knew what they were thinking. And He did something He did a lot in the Gospels. He referenced a story from the Scriptures.

> *He said to them, "You will surely say this proverb to Me, 'Physician, heal yourself! Whatever we have heard done in Capernaum, do also here in Your country.'" Then He said, "Assuredly, I say to you, no prophet is accepted in his own country.*

But I tell you truly, many widows were in Israel in the days of Elijah, when the heaven was shut up three years and six months, and there was a great famine throughout all the land; but to none of them was Elijah sent except to Zarephath, in the region of Sidon, to a woman who was a widow. And many lepers were in Israel in the time of Elisha the prophet, and none of them was cleansed except Naaman the Syrian."

So all those in the synagogue, when they heard these things, were filled with wrath, and rose up and thrust Him out of the city; and they led Him to the brow of the hill on which their city was built, that they might throw Him down over the cliff. Then passing through the midst of them, He went His way (Luke 4:23-30).

Now, I've read that passage many times, and each time I've wondered what made them so angry they wanted to throw Jesus off a cliff. You see, Jesus had a way of answering questions where He didn't answer the question directly. Instead, He made an inference here. He was saying that the people of God are forever missing the blessing of God. In Elijah's time there were many widows in Israel, and Elijah wasn't sent to any of them. He was sent to a foreigner over in Sidon. And there were many lepers in Israel in the time of Elisha—and none of them were cleansed except Naaman the Syrian. The foreigner—the one not familiar with the prophet.

> The people of God are forever missing the blessing of God.

Jesus knew exactly what He was doing when He mentioned those stories. He knew they would be furious. And they were; they tried to throw Him off of a cliff. If ever a city blew an opportunity, it was Nazareth. Had they welcomed Him and honored Him, He may have based His ministry there. It was His hometown after all, and His mother still lived there. Instead, He went to Capernaum and set up shop—and Capernaum got the blessing. All because they wouldn't honor Him, and all because they thought they knew Him. They didn't recognize this renewed Jesus who had been freshly immersed and empowered with the Holy Spirit for ministry.

Jesus said in John 6:63, "It is the Spirit who gives life; the flesh profits nothing. The words that I speak to you are spirit, and they are life." When we look positively, in faith, to the things of the Spirit, it generates hope and faith in us, which leads to belief, which leads to miracles. When we look in the natural (1 Corinthians 2:14) it leads us into the flesh, leading to no faith, leading to unbelief, leading to no miracles.

So, why were no widows in Israel helped in Elijah's time? They were not looking to words of the Spirit that would bring them life. Why were no lepers healed in Elisha's time? Again, they were not looking to words of the Spirit that would bring them hope, leading to faith, leading to the miracles of God. Honoring the anointing leads to being in the Spirit, which leads to faith, which leads to miracles. Dishonoring the anointing leads to the flesh, which leads to unbelief, which leads to no miracles.

Have you ever heard the phrase *familiarity breeds contempt*? It seems to happen that when we know someone well, or at least we think we do, we tend to only know him or her in the flesh, not in the Spirit. When we've walked with people for a long time, we know all the dirt on them, so to speak, and so we can decide they don't deserve honor. But then the "anointed" speaker comes to town, maybe Bill Johnson or Randy Clark or Heidi Baker. We find it easy to honor them, because we really don't know any of their faults or weaknesses. But the Holy Spirit who resides and works in Bill Johnson or Randy Clark or Heidi or John and Carol also resides and works in the leaders around you. If you can honor the anointing that Bill or Randy carry, then you can honor the anointing of leaders around you.

Naaman the Leper

Jesus referenced the story of Naaman the Syrian, saying that there were many lepers in Israel and living in Samaria in the time of Elisha, the prophet, and none of them were cleansed. Not one. Now, Elisha was one of the most anointed men of God ever, so why were none of the lepers around him healed?

The story is told in 2 Kings 5. Naaman is the commander of the Syrian army, and he has a problem—he has leprosy. The Syrians had gone out on a raid in Israel and brought back a little girl, who now serves Naaman's wife. This little girl is fascinating; here she is, kidnapped and brought to a strange country, and she isn't filled with bitterness and hate; instead, she says, *"If only my master were with the prophet who is in Samaria! For he would heal him of his leprosy"* (2 Kings 5:3). She tells this man who had made her a slave how he could get well.

Imagine what Naaman has been through with this disease. He has probably tried everything imaginable to cure it and probably spent loads of money on doctors and treatments. So when the girl tells him about the prophet, he leaps at the opportunity. It sounds a bit like a long shot, but he goes for it. That's faith. That's determination. He goes and tells the king of Syria what this little girl had said (can you just imagine taking the word of a child to the king? How desperate was Naaman?), and the king agrees to send a letter to the king of Israel.

So off they go, Naaman and his entourage, carrying a fortune in gold and silver to honor the king of Israel. But when they get there, the king of Israel thinks Syria is picking a fight with him. The king tears his clothes and has a bit of a fit. When Elisha finds out about all of this, he sends word to the king, saying, *"Why have you torn your clothes? Please let him come to me, and he shall know that there is a prophet in Israel"* (2 Kings 5:8). Elisha is not boasting here. He's not claiming, "I'm the man. Send him over here, and I'll show him who's anointed." No, he's just telling the truth. He is a prophet, and he knows what he carries. He knows what he can do for this sick man. He's proclaiming the truth and honoring the anointing on his life.

Naaman comes to Elisha's house with his entourage and knocks on the door. But Elisha himself doesn't come to the door; instead, he sends one of his servant boys to give Naaman instructions. *"Go and wash in the Jordan seven times, and your flesh shall be restored to you, and you shall be clean"* (2 Kings 5:10).

The story goes that Naaman storms off in a rage. Here he's humbled himself, coming before the king, bringing gifts and gold—and the guy tells him to go take a bath? Naaman grumbles, *"Indeed, I said to myself, 'He will surely come out to me, and stand and call on the name of the Lord his God, and wave his hand over the place, and heal the leprosy"* (2 Kings 5:11). In other words, "I thought he would come out here himself to greet *me.* I thought he would have some magic that would fix my problem. Doesn't he know who I am?"

But Naaman has good friends around him, friends who understand who Elisha is. They answer him, saying, *"My father, if the prophet had told you to do something great, would you not have done it? How much more then, when he says to you, 'Wash and be clean'?"* (2 Kings 5:13).

Can you imagine the turmoil in Naaman's mind? He knows that his men haven't really seen the extent of the leprosy. He knows what he looks like, and the request to bathe himself comes at a sharp price—his dignity. His pride. In order to do what the prophet said, he is going to have to humble himself and do what this prophet—whom he hasn't even seen in person—says.

So down to the river he goes. If you haven't seen the Jordan River, it's not very wide and it's very muddy, and the banks are slippery. There's really no dignified way to get in and out of it, even if you don't have leprosy. Naaman, stripped out of his commander's uniform, with his leprosy fully on display, goes down into the river, and comes out again.

No change.

He does it again.

No change.

And again.

No change.

Can you imagine what's going through his head at this point? "You idiot. How could you believe that know-nothing prophet? You've just made a total fool of yourself in front of your men—and in front of the Syrian soldiers."

But despite those thoughts, he goes down into the river. Six times he goes under, and there is no change. But on the seventh time, all of a sudden his leprous skin becomes as smooth as a child's; the leprosy is gone.

Naaman eventually honored the anointing of the prophet by obeying the word of the Lord through him despite the indignity and embarrassment it must have caused him. Even when it didn't seem to be working, he kept at it—because the prophet said so. And he was healed.

Why weren't the lepers in Israel healed? It may be that they thought they knew Elisha, that they had seen him fight with his wife or not mow his lawn or, you know, that time when he was younger and had too much to drink that one time. He can't have any real authority; he can't *really* be a man of God because he's too normal. Only those special people have the real anointing. And the lepers weren't healed.

Repent for Dishonor

We need to repent for those times we've dishonored pastors and leaders. "Why can't he/she be more like Kathryn Kuhlman/Bill Johnson/etc.? Who does he think he is, driving that car/living in that house/taking that vacation? I can't receive anything from someone who would do/say those things." How often do we miss out on an impartation because we dishonor the one who has what we need through criticism and complaining?

There's one more anointed person we often dishonor, and that is ourselves. We say things to ourselves like, "I know I was baptized in the Holy Spirit and everything, but I could never do what Carol Arnott or Heidi Baker does. I could never see healing." "I've never been to Bible school." "I'm too old, or I'm too young." We make excuses, and we disqualify ourselves. As much as we know other people's shortcomings, we are painfully familiar with our own, and we just know God could never use us *that* way.

> " How often do we miss out on an impartation because we dishonor the one who has what we need through criticism and complaining? "

Have you minimized your own anointing? Have you missed out on what God wants to do in and through you because you don't honor the Spirit who lives in you and on you? Why not repent now? Ask God to forgive you for that. He's so ready to work in you and through you, but you have to give honor to your own anointing and decide to get the necessary training and go for it!

"But that sounds like pride," you say. Carol loves to tell a story about a donkey who goes in and out of Jerusalem, day after day after day. One day, he comes home, full of pride and strutting around the stable. He tells his mother, "Mom, I'm really special. I mean, I'm really something, Mom. You have no idea what happened today."

His mom answers, "What's with you?"

The little donkey says, "Today they were throwing palm branches in front of me. They were waving and throwing their coats in front of me. They were shouting, 'Hosanna to the king.'"

His wise mom says, "Son, I hate to burst your bubble, but it wasn't you they were exalting. It was the one you were carrying."

> " We honor them because of who and what they carry—the anointing of the Holy Spirit. "

Read Luke 4:18-19 again, but this time apply that scripture to yourself.

The Spirit of the Lord is upon Me, Because He has anointed Me To preach the gospel to the poor; He has sent Me to heal the brokenhearted, to proclaim liberty to the captives and recovery of sight to the blind, to set at liberty those who are oppressed, to proclaim the acceptable year of the Lord.

Honoring the anointing works just like that. Second Corinthians 5:16 says that we no longer regard anyone according to the flesh; instead, we honor them because of who and what they carry—the anointing of the Holy Spirit.

ACTIVATE

Could you sense Him as you read this chapter? I believe that some of you got a fresh anointing even as you were reading, didn't you? Well, if you didn't, there's no time like the present! Just stop right now. Thank Him for His presence. Ask Him to pour out fresh oil, fresh wine, fresh fire on you. Fire on you! More, Lord!

NOTE

1. John Piper, "The Place of the Holy Spirit in the Trinity," Desiring God, February 16, 1987, http://www.desiringgod .org/articles/the-place-of-the-holy-spirit-in -the-trinity.

Chapter 8

The Glory

For the earth will be filled with the knowledge of
the glory of the Lord, as the waters cover the sea.
—HABAKKUK 2:14

PEOPLE OFTEN ASK WHAT ACTUALLY HAPPENED WHEN THE HOLY Spirit fell on us in 1994. After all, there had been plenty of other meetings and plenty of other pastors who had seen things like we were seeing; laughter, shaking, falling down, speaking in tongues—these are all things that have characterized revival throughout church history. What made our meeting that night with Randy Clark different?

When we talk about what makes a revival, of course there are all kinds of definitions. There are all kinds of ways the Holy Spirit can—and has—shown up at various times. For us at the time, we didn't know right away that this would become a "revival"; we simply knew it was the visitation of the Holy Spirit we had been so hungry for because it was so deeply satisfying to the hearts and souls of so many.

When God Shows Up

I believe God shows up in lots of ways. For us, it looked like people not being able to stand up under the power. It looked like uncontrollable laughter breaking out. It looked like a roomful of people speaking in languages they hadn't learned.

In 2011, a glory cloud appeared during a service at Bethel Church in Redding, California. This cloud looked like smoke and glitter, and it hung around in one part of the room for quite a while. Was it the presence of God? Of course it was. It was His glory, physically manifested in the room where people were worshiping Him.

What will happen when this next wave hits? What will happen when the glory comes? What will it look like? How will it impact the world around us?

The Nations

As of 2015, Christians made up the largest religious group in the world, about a third of the world's population.[1] In China, one of the most difficult places to be a Christian, some conservative estimates say there are as many as 60 million Christians gathering and worshiping in the underground churches.[2] Additionally, there are millions more in the "legal" Three Self churches of China. Voice of the Martyrs (VOM) Canada reports that there are "thousands upon thousands coming to Christ" in Iran.[3]

Although some reports say there are places where Christianity is on the decline, more evidence would show that the Gospel is spreading throughout the world, with thousands upon thousands coming to know Jesus in many, many nations.

> The Gospel is spreading throughout the world, with thousands upon thousands coming to know Jesus in many, many nations.

Persecution of believers is also on the rise. VOM reports:

> Iran remains one of the most difficult nations in the world in which to be a Christian. Since President Hassan Rouhani took office in August 2013, the number of individuals in prison because of their beliefs has increased, and Christians are especially targeted. Over the past year, Iranian authorities have raided church services, threatened church members and arrested and imprisoned worshipers and church leaders, particularly Christian converts from Islam. Currently, there are approximately 90 Christians either in prison or awaiting trial.[4]

North Korea remains one of the most dangerous places to be a Christian; if arrested, believers face imprisonment, torture, and even death. And yet, there are believers in North Korea, and evidence that the church there is growing. Muslims in Turkey and Iraq and other Middle Eastern nations are reporting dreams where Jesus shows up and tells them exactly who He is and what they must do to be saved.

Signposts

What does this tell us about revival and the next wave? Before a tsunami occurs, there are signs that point to the event. Scientists have ways of predicting where and when the phenomenon will occur. These two things together—both a growing number of believers as well as the rise of persecution—act in much the same way: predictors of a coming tsunami wave of revival.

In their book *Waves of Revival,* Fred and Sharon Wright point to two components of a major revival; one is an emphasis on "essential truths about the nature and purposes of God that have been ignored, discarded or lost by successive generations of professing believers, well-meaning church leaders, and theologians."[5] In other words, the tsunami serves to bring the church back on track. We'll talk more about that in the next chapter.

Invited to a Wedding

This coming revival, we believe, will help to usher in the second coming of Jesus—the Bridegroom coming for His Bride. The latter part of the book of Revelation describes a wedding; Revelation 19:7 tells us that the *"marriage of the Lamb has come."* We're getting ready for a wedding.

When a couple is engaged and preparing for marriage, the days and weeks and months leading up to the wedding day are full of busy preparations—making arrangements, finding the right dress, ordering flowers, registering for and receiving gifts to set up housekeeping. Lots of exciting things happen in that time.

Whenever I'm around couples who are engaged to be married, I notice something—a desire to be with one another. A desire to talk, to hold hands, to get to know one another; a desire to be intimate with one another; almost a hunger for the wedding day to finally arrive.

They tell everyone about their beloved. "Have you met him/her?" they will ask. "Well, let me tell you all about this person I love so much." Sometimes it's difficult to get them to change the subject.

According to Fred and Sharon, the second component is that revival is spurred on by "hungry and desperate people."[6] It is spurred on by a people so desperately in love, so hungry for more, that they can't talk about anything else. They can't focus on anything else. Their Bridegroom is on the way, and they want everyone to know it.

> Revival is spurred on by a people so desperately in love, so hungry for more, that they can't talk about anything else. They can't focus on anything else. Their Bridegroom is on the way, and they want everyone to know it.

Signs of Revival

We are often asked, how will we know when the next wave gets here? What will it look like when it shows up? Throughout history, each wave of revival is characterized by a few things. First of all, what we would call the manifestations of the Holy Spirit seem to be consistent throughout each revival—early

Anabaptists were known for falling down under the anointing; John Wesley felt a "warming" in his heart at the presence of the Holy Spirit; many at Azusa Street spoke in other tongues.

When the Spirit fell on us in 1994, we had an outbreak of laughter, of shaking, of falling to the floor. It's still happening, both in Toronto at Catch the Fire and now all around the world, as those who have been touched by the revival spread the joy to their home countries and hometowns.

Second, all of these waves of revival were characterized by healing and deliverance. In 1727, the Moravians began a 100-year-long prayer meeting in which hundreds were healed. In 1894, Smith Wigglesworth was overcome by the Spirit, which led to a healing ministry that spread around the world for the better part of 30 years. In the 20-plus years of our revival, we've seen cancers healed, limbs grow out, and deaf ears opened. Heidi Baker's ministry, which was sparked in large part by her visit to Toronto in 1997, has seen thousands healed in Africa.

Impact on Society

Revival also affects society at large in that it sparks a passion for justice. Out of the revival birthed through John Wesley came a young man named William Wilberforce who, empowered by the Spirit, would see the abolition of slavery in England during his lifetime.

Our friends Bill and Beni Johnson pastor Bethel Church in Redding, California. Recently, the city of Redding was in a bit of a budget crunch and wasn't going to be able to pay some of their fire and police personnel. Bethel Church paid a large sum of money to the city to help Redding keep their staffing intact. I know this flows out of Bill and Beni's Holy Spirit-empowered way of thinking.

Finally, revival sparks a desire to see those who don't know Jesus as their Savior brought into the family. Evangelism flourishes during times of revival; ours has been no different. It's as if those who have fallen in love and are anticipating a wedding want everyone else to come too.

> " Those who have fallen in love and are anticipating a wedding want everyone else to come too. "

To See Jesus Glorified

The point of revival isn't the manifestations of the Spirit, although we certainly enjoy them. It's not to have nightly meetings for 12 years, although we enjoyed that too. The point of revival is simply to see Jesus glorified in the earth. When He is lifted up, all people will be drawn to Him (see John 12:32). As the wave of revival rises over the earth, the name of Jesus is brought to light once again.

Surrounding each revival was an emphasis on a particular characteristic of God. In the Reformation, we saw the restoration of the truth that Jesus Christ is the only way to salvation. During the First Great Awakening, we saw the restoration of the importance of the Great Commission. In the Pentecostal Revival, we saw the restoration of the emphasis on the Holy Spirit. And during the Father Heart Revival (Toronto), we saw the restoration of the absolute truth of God's Father heart and desire for intimacy with us, His children.

We believe this next great tsunami wave of revival will be about the Bridegroom and His Bride, that it will serve as the invitation to a wedding—*to the Wedding.* To the Marriage Supper of the Lamb.

You see, even though Christians make up the largest religious group in the world, it's still not everyone. Billions of people still don't know the love of their heavenly Father. They don't know that they are sons and daughters of a King—*of the King.* They don't know that He desperately wants to heal their hearts, bodies, and relationships. They don't know that He desires to be their source of truth, their source of joy, their source of peace. They don't know that they are invited to a wedding where they get to be joined in oneness forever to the most beautiful, most faithful, most wonderful Bridegroom there has ever been. We believe that this next wave of revival will serve as an invitation to that wedding.

We Haven't Seen Anything Yet

This revival will be characterized by a global harvest of souls. In this age of air travel and technology, there is almost no people group that hasn't already been reached for the Gospel. When Heidi and Rolland went to Mozambique over 20 years ago, there were several tribes in the north that were categorized as unreached people groups, and many across the region had never heard the name of Jesus. Heidi and Rolland, empowered by the Holy Spirit and full of the Father's love for the people, have spent their time, energy, and resources taking the message of a loving heavenly Father out into the "bush bush"—the remotest places in Mozambique—several times a week. In the years since they began this journey, thousands upon thousands of people have heard the Gospel message and received salvation.

We know that there are still places and people who haven't heard this message of love. We know that there are still billions who have heard but have rejected it. That's okay; Jesus loves them too. As many as will go into unevangelized places, many will go to those who have heard and have not yet believed. After all, we're inviting people to a party.

What will it look like? I think it will look familiar in some ways. When the infinite God of the universe encounters a finite being such as us,

> " We believe the glory of the latter house will be greater than the former. This revival will eclipse what happened in the book of Acts— the greatest revival to date. "

things tend to happen. We tend to respond. But I also believe that as David Ruis prophesied so many years ago, we haven't seen anything yet. We believe the glory of the latter house will be greater than the former. This revival will eclipse what happened in the book of Acts—the greatest revival to date.

The Bride Prepares

What does an invitation to a wedding, especially a wedding like this, look like? Revelation 19:7 says, *"Let us rejoice and exult and give him the glory, for the marriage of the Lamb has come, and his Bride has made herself ready"* (ESV). It looks like His Bride readying herself for her coming Bridegroom.

A Bride readies herself for her groom by setting herself apart. She is preparing for the consummation of a growing intimacy, and she spends months preparing herself. Brides can get so focused on the upcoming marriage that they lose sight of every other thing in their lives.

Jesus Himself actually told us how to prepare.

> *Then the kingdom of heaven shall be likened to ten virgins who took their lamps and went out to meet the bridegroom. Now five of them were wise, and five were foolish. Those who were foolish took their lamps and took no oil with them, but the wise took oil in their vessels with their lamps. But while the bridegroom was delayed, they all slumbered and slept. And at midnight a cry was heard: "Behold, the bridegroom is coming; go out to meet him!" Then all those virgins arose and trimmed their lamps. And the foolish said to the wise, "Give us some of your oil, for our lamps are going out." But the wise answered, saying, "No, lest there should not be enough for us and you; but go rather to those who sell, and buy for yourselves." And while they went to buy, the bridegroom came, and those who were ready went in with him to the wedding;*

and the door was shut. Afterward the other virgins came also, saying, "Lord, Lord, open to us." But he answered and said, "Assuredly, I say to you, I do not know you." Watch therefore, for you know neither the day nor the hour in which the Son of Man is coming (Matthew 25:1-13).

In early February of 1994, I (Carol) had a dramatic vision about this parable.

We were receiving prayer in a meeting because we were about to leave on a missions trip to Hungary. I was on the platform, and I fell down under the power of the Holy Spirit. I began stomping my feet as if I were running. Then my legs went up in the air, and I began shouting and waving my arms around. What a distraction.

Someone was trying to preach at this point, and John told me there were people in the room wondering, *Why isn't anybody moving that poor woman off the platform? She's embarrassing herself. Doesn't anybody care about her dignity? Not to mention the distraction she's causing.*

John knew me well enough to know that God was doing something profound. "Absolutely nobody touch her. Leave her there and let it happen. I don't want to interfere with what God is doing."

At the end of this encounter, I got back on my feet and tried my best to explain what had just happened, what Jesus had just shown to me. I'd been dancing in meadows with Him. There were magnificent flowers, and I saw the glory of Heaven in all its beauty. I walked with Jesus along streets of gold on the way to a spectacular banquet hall, filled with ornate tables set with crystal and gold. It was unbelievable.

I asked the Lord, "What should I do with all this?"

Jesus said, "I want you to tell My people that the banquet feast is almost prepared, and they must be like the five wise virgins so they will be full of oil at My coming."

It was a life-changing encounter for me and remains the strongest vision I've ever had.

After Carol had that vision, I (John) kept thinking about it. I read the story of the virgins over and over and meditated on it. I asked the Lord, "What are You trying to show us?"

The ten virgins are all waiting for Jesus the Bridegroom to return, and the virgins are often seen as a representation of the church. Each one had a lamp, which represented their witness and ministry as believers. They waited for the Lord's return, but He was delayed. Five of them were wise and brought extra oil with them, and five were foolish because they did not.

The Oil of Intimacy

As I asked the Lord about this, He showed me that the oil is a very important element of this story—it represents the Holy Spirit in the context of intimacy. This can be seen in what the bridegroom says to the five unwise virgins when they come knocking at the end of the parable: *"Assuredly, I say to you, I do not know you"* (Matt. 25:12).

I looked up the word *know* in Greek, expecting to find the word *ginosko*. In fact, the word *know* in this passage is the word *oida,* a form of the verb *eido. Ginosko* is most commonly associated with knowledge that is progressively attained, such as through learning. In this context, it would mean, "I do not know you. I have not learned the information about you." However, the word *oida,* while similar, is often used as "to know something perfectly, completely, or by perception." It has a much more intimate connotation and is often translated "to see."

In this verse, it means, "I have not seen you. We have not looked into one another's eyes. We have not sat face to face with one another and exchanged intimate glances." What it really means is we don't have intimacy with one another.

In preparing for the next wave of glory, our primary task is to keep the wicks of our lamps from burning out. The way we do that is by making sure we have enough oil, enough intimacy with the Lord through the Holy Spirit, to keep our fires burning.

Isn't that exactly how a bride would prepare to meet her bridegroom? She would make sure she was truly getting to know him, truly seeing him in face-to-face encounters. When John and I (Carol) were dating, we lived about an hour and a half away from each other. We would often meet halfway and spend the evening holding hands across a restaurant table, gazing into each other's eyes and telling each other how much we wanted to be together. We were preparing for marriage.

> As lovers of Jesus who are preparing for our final wedding with Him, we should be spending lots of time gazing into His eyes, with Him gazing into ours.

As lovers of Jesus who are preparing for our final wedding with Him, we should be spending lots of time gazing into His eyes, with Him gazing into ours. We should tell Him over and over again how much we love to be with Him and how we can't wait to be one with Him forever—and hear Him say all those things to us.

This revival will be one that ignites a fire for intimacy with the Lord. It will ignite a passion to see our oil lamps fully ready for His coming, so that when He does come for the Marriage Supper, He will say, "Come with Me, My Bride. I know you. I see you. We have spent so much time face to face with each other, that I knew you the minute I saw you. Let's go and be one forever."

And we will be so in love with Him that we will invite everyone we know to experience the same intimacy with Him. We will spread His love to China and Iran and Turkey and North Korea and Africa, and billions will come to know Him—and to love Him.

ACTIVATE

One of the songs that we sang repeatedly in the early days of the Toronto Revival went like this: "Let Your glory fall in this room; let it go forth from here to the nations! Let Your fragrance rest in this place, as we gather to seek Your face!"[7] Why not pray that right now? Sing it if you know the tune. If not, just pray the words. God, let Your glory fall so that we can be a light to the nations! We want revival on the earth, God! We want the earth to be filled with the fragrance of Your presence!

NOTES

1. Conrad Hackett and David McClendon, "Christians Remain World's Largest Religious Group, but They Are Declining in Europe," Pew Research Center, April 05, 2017, http://www.pewresearch.org/fact-tank/2017/04/05/christians-remain-worlds-largest-religious-group-but-they-are-declining-in-europe/.

2. Ian Johnson, "In China, Unregistered Churches Are Driving a Religious Revolution," *The Atlantic,* April 23, 2017, https://www.theatlantic.com/international/archive/2017/04/china-unregistered-churches-driving-religious-revolution/521544/.

3. ChristianPost.com, "Thousands of Muslims Reportedly Turning to Christ in Middle East," Fox News, January 11, 2017, http://www.foxnews.com/world/2017/01/11/thousands-muslims-reportedly-turning-to-christ-in-middle-east.html.

4. "Iran," The Voice of the Martyrs, accessed August 17, 2017, http://www.persecution.com/public/prayermap.aspx?clickfrom=%3d6d61696e5f6d656e75.

5. Fred and Sharon Wright, *Waves of Revival* (Toronto, Canada: Catch the Fire Books, 2015), 23.

6   Ibid., 23.

7. David Ruis, "Let Your Glory Fall," copyright © 1993 Mercy/Vineyard Publishing. All rights reserved. International copyright secured.

Chapter 9

The Warning

IN THEIR BOOK *WAVES OF REVIVAL*, FRED AND SHARON WRIGHT describe the two primary components of a tsunami revival. We've already discussed one of those components at length, that "revival is spurred on by hungry and desperate people who are seeking answers to their needs, the church's needs, and the needs in society."[1] We are hungry, God!

The other primary feature of a revival such as this is that "it emphasizes essential truths about the nature and purposes of God that have been ignored, discarded or lost by successive generations of professing believers, well-meaning church leaders, and theologians."[2] In other words, the revival serves as a course correction for the church itself.

We believe there are things in our society that absolutely need a course correction. But as God will work through the church to achieve that correction, our first focus needs to be on ourselves as believers. Where have we gotten off course? What needs to be set right?

The Dream

My (Carol's) birthday was on a Sunday a couple of years ago. John was out of town, and my son was going to pick me up that morning and take me to church. Well, the night before Mike phoned and said he had gotten called in to work and wouldn't be able to take me. I already wasn't feeling well, and I was disappointed.

Before I went to bed that Saturday night, I told the Lord that if He wanted me to go to church on Sunday, He was going to have to wake me up. I wasn't going to set my alarm.

That night, I had a dream. I've only shared this dream a couple of times, but I feel that it's so important to the body of Christ.

In the dream, I was standing at the front of our church, down on the floor right in front of the stage, worshiping. All of a sudden, I was caught up in a whirlwind that took me up, up, up to the ceiling. I thought, "God, am I going through the roof?"

And then I came down, and stood right by the podium. I don't really know what happened; something either came on me or came off of me. It was like a cloak, and it was heavy. I grabbed the microphone from the stand, and I spoke to the people.

I said, "The Lord is saying, 'There's another cloud—a cloud of holiness. It will not be a cloud of outward, good behavior holiness, but it will be a cloud of My holiness—the reverent fear of the Lord, which is the beginning of wisdom.'"

I began to say to our congregation, and I'm saying it to you right now, that there has been such an outpouring of grace for the past 20-plus years. Unspeakable grace. Incredible, beautiful grace. But some of you have used that grace to do your own thing, to think, *Well, the Lord won't really be upset about that thing I did because He's so merciful and so loving. I'll come back and repent, and everything will be all right.*

Or He's been asking you to do something, and you've said, "Well, He won't really mind if I don't do that. He's so full of grace."

> "When that glory cloud comes down, when that next wave hits, you better have your heart right. Get right with Me."

I tell you, *He minds.* He minds. He has been giving us mercy so that we can get our hearts healed. He has been giving us so much grace; He has been pouring out love on the wounded places of our hearts, and we've seen so much healing. But now we're saying we want more. We're saying, "I want what You have, Jesus. I want to do what You do, Jesus. I want the greater works."

And the Lord said, "When that glory cloud comes down, when that next wave hits, you better have your heart right. Get right with Me. Stop playing with sin and excusing it!"

In the dream, I saw the glory cloud start to come down. I said to the congregation, "The altar of mercy is open. Those of you who want to get your hearts right, those of you who have been taking advantage of unsanctified mercy, run. Run to the altar. There is repentance at the altar. There is forgiveness at the altar. But to those of you who still want to play the game of, 'God won't mind if I sin!' I say *run. Get out of here.* I fear for your very life."

Then I saw, in the back of the sanctuary, risers. And I thought, *That's odd. We don't have risers.* I felt the Lord told me to go back. There were two men sitting on the bleachers, both of them in three-piece suits and ties. They sat with their arms crossed, talking to one another and laughing—and pointing at me. Mocking me.

People were streaming forward toward the altar, and I headed through the crowd toward the men. I got about three quarters of the way down the aisle toward the back and was just a few feet away from the men when suddenly, both of them fell off of the risers onto the floor and lay there, motionless. I wondered if they were out under the power of the Spirit—or if they were dead.

I started to move toward them, and God said, "No, don't go to them. See that young man at the other door?" I looked, and there was a young man there. He was running part way up toward the stage, and then he would turn and run back toward the door. He kept running up and back, up and back. "Go to him."

I went over to the young man and said, "Young man, the Lord has a calling on your life. He has given you a gift that you had been walking in. But right now, the Lord is saying that you are in secret sin. You are having an affair with your secretary. The Lord says, 'Run to the altar right now, because I have not lifted that calling. I will restore you and I will heal you. But if you walk out that door, I fear that you might become like Lot's wife.'"

And with that, I woke up.

After the Dream

I looked over at the clock and it was a quarter to ten. We live a half an hour from the church, and church starts at 10:30 a.m. I thought, *Oh well, I've missed church. Okay Lord, I must write down this dream.*

Our bed sits a little high up, so I slid off. As soon as I put my foot on the floor, the Lord said "Carol"—in an audible, loud voice. Now, I've only heard the audible voice of the Lord one other time, when I got saved. (He spoke the entire 23rd Psalm to me in a bathroom.)

"Carol." He said. "Carol, get into the shower; wash your hair. Get your makeup on. Get dressed. Get something to eat, and get down to the church—*now.*"

Well, I'm telling you, all of my excuses went out the window in a hurry. I've never moved so fast in all my life. As quickly as I could, I got dressed and got out the door into the car.

Now, I knew I needed to get the dream written down somehow. I'm not very "techy," so it took me a few minutes to find the "record" function on my iPhone. I'm driving with one hand, trying to get the dream recorded, and praying that every one of the ten or so lights between our house and the church would be *green*. I may have been driving just a little fast, too. (If you're reading this and you're a police officer, I'm so sorry.) Finally, with much prayer, I got the record function to work and I managed to dictate the dream onto my phone.

I got to the church and looked at the clock; it was 10:50. I wondered where I would park, but lo and behold, my parking space was still wide open. I whipped into my parking space and got out of the car. Then I thought, "Oh, where am I going to sit?"

At first I thought I would sit in the back. But I don't like to sit in the back. Then I thought I would sit with the worship team. There's always a seat there. I started to walk up the aisle and the Lord said, very sternly, *You go sit in your own seat.*

I said, "Lord, there might be people sitting there."

He said, just as sternly, "Then tell them to *move.*"

Gulp.

I rounded the corner at the end of the aisle and headed toward my usual seat. I have no idea who the two people were who were sitting where John and I usually sit, but they took one look at my face and fled. I have no idea what I must have looked like at that point.

I sat down, and Sandra (Long) looked at me and said, "I think you must have something to share today."

And then it hit me. "Lord, are we doing the dream today?"

He said, "No, not today. Today is a test of your obedience."

Getting Our Hearts Right Before God

You see, the Lord is calling us. He's calling us to get our hearts right before Him. I want you to stop right now and examine yourself. Is there anything in your heart that comes before Jesus? Is it your church? Is it your work? Is it your ministry? How much do we really want the *more?* How hungry are we really?

In the dream, God told me that people had sins in their lives, things where they thought, *Oh, the Lord won't mind.* Or maybe you didn't think that. Maybe the things in your life aren't the *really big* sins; but maybe they are things that keep you from putting Jesus first.

> How much do we really want the *more?* How hungry are we really?

Jesus is calling us to be a holy people, set apart unto Him. He is a jealous God, and He desires that He would come first in our lives.

We are about to move into this next wave of revival, which I really believe will be the wave that gets us ready for His coming. I believe we are looking at the end times. Have you watched the news? We hear about wars and rumors of wars, just like Scripture says. Have you been following Israel? What's happening in Israel is prophetically pointing toward what's about to happen. It's closer than we think.

I know that no one knows the day or the hour. But He says, "I'll show you signs. I'll show you things in the heavens and in the earth." Luke 21 tells us that there will be signs in the sun, moon, and stars (see Luke 21:25). In 2014 and 2015 there were four what we call "blood moons." This is a very rare phenomenon, where four lunar eclipses happen very close together. (They are often called "blood moons" because the way the light refracts during the eclipse makes the moon look sort of reddish.)

These four eclipses all took place on Jewish feast days during those two years. The last two times this has happened were on the Passover following the establishment of Israel as a nation in 1948, and again in 1967, the year of the Six-Day War against Israel—which, incidentally, Israel won.

More recently, we have had a solar eclipse across America, followed by a string of damaging hurricanes, out of control wildfires on the west coast, and powerfully destructive earthquakes in Mexico.

> " What's happening in Israel is prophetically pointing toward what's about to happen. It's closer than we think. "

But great blessings are coming also. We are aware that the anointing is increasing, day by day. We are watching the nation of Israel very closely. The first rumblings of a tsunami often occur way underground, where only those with ears to hear can detect them.

The time is at hand. It's going to be soon; it's so close. Is your heart ready? This is a holy time. We want our hearts purified and ready for this fresh move of the Holy Spirit.

How Do We Get Ready?

There are a couple of ways we need to prepare ourselves. The first way, just like in my dream, is that God wants us to deal with our secret sins, the ones we think nobody knows about. God knows. You may think you're hiding those things, but God already knows everything in your heart. Those things will trip you up. They will be distractions. They will be things that keep you from really pressing into the next outpouring.

But God has offered you mercy. He's inviting you to the altar of His presence where you can repent of those things and be forgiven. Take some time today and do business with God. Ask Him to root out those things that have crept in.

The second way we need to get ready is to deal with grace. God is so gracious. He offers us a way out of our mess, no matter how bad it is. But so many these days are taking advantage of God's kindness, using it as an excuse to sin. *Well, God has to forgive me,* someone might think. *It's grace.* Or even more, some might not obey what they know God has told them to do, thinking He'll just be okay with it.

Others even call sin "good," claiming that what God has called unholy is holy. They refuse to repent, claiming they have nothing to repent for. This is dangerous, church.

Hyper Grace

There is a movement within the church body at large today that would take the wonderful grace of God and turn it into an illegal distortion. In a nutshell, this movement teaches that because you were once saved, once cleansed by the blood of Jesus, you never need to do it again. You never need to repent again for anything. It takes the tender compassion of the Father and turns it into a license to sin, missing the mark completely.

This is dangerous, church. Of course we understand that Jesus's blood atoned for all our sin—past, yours and mine, present and future. This is what we call "justification."

But, *"Shall we continue in sin that grace may abound? Certainly not!"* (Rom. 6:1-2). And, *"What then? Shall we sin because we are not under law but under grace?"* Certainly not! (Rom. 6:15). But sometimes I still sin! I don't want to, but I do. I still do things that miss the mark that I know I shouldn't do. I still do things that I need to repent of—and be forgiven for. This is what we call "sanctification." The Bible teaches that I have been saved, I am being saved, and I will be saved. In other words, my salvation was completed when I received Jesus as my Lord and Savior. But according to Philippians 2:12, I am also to *"work out your own salvation with fear and trembling."* You owe it to yourself to have a really good study of the book of Romans, especially chapters 6, 7, and 8. It teaches that by the grace of our Lord Jesus Christ, we can be overcomers and live victorious lives.

Although my identity is secure in the fact that I am no longer a sinner, I still sin from time to time. I still need to come to the cross and once again confess my need for His cleansing and forgiveness. I still need to repent on an ongoing basis.

> We are called to be continually sanctified. We are called to be holy, even as God is holy.

The primary danger in a hyper-grace teaching such as this is that it will be used as a license to sin. "I can do whatever I want, because God has already forgiven me!" May it never be! We are called to be continually sanctified. We are saved *from* our sins, not *in* our sins. Sanctification is a progressive process. We are called to be holy, even as God is holy.

A Holiness Revival

Both Patricia King and Stacey Campbell have prophesied concerning this coming wave of revival. It will be a holiness revival, a reformation revival. It will bring about a much-needed course correction within the church. Smith Wigglesworth prophesied 70 years ago (as of this writing) in 1947 that the final revival would be one of the Word and the Spirit together. As we return to honoring the clear teaching of the Word of God, including holiness until the Lord comes, we can expect to see the Holy Spirit moving like never before. Jesus said that mankind shall live by every word that proceeds out of the mouth of God (see Matt. 4:4).

This next wave of revival will be one of holiness, of purity, of being set apart. That's what holiness means: "set apart." In Romans 12:1, it says, *"I beseech you therefore, brethren, by the mercies of God, that you present your bodies a living sacrifice, holy, acceptable to God, which is your reasonable service."* That word *holy* means "dedicated to God." It also means to be "morally and spiritually excellent."

> We have been invited into an intimate love affair with Jesus. I love Him. And when I am in love, I don't want anything to come between us.

Now, we know that the Gospel is not a "good behavior" Gospel. If it were, we wouldn't have needed Jesus to die and rise again; we could have handled it ourselves. Jesus is the One who purifies us, who makes us clean. But we have a part to play too.

We have been invited into an intimate love affair with Jesus. I love Him. And when I am in love, I don't want anything to come between us.

John and I have been married for many years. He loves me unconditionally. But if I did things that he didn't want me to do, especially things that would hurt him or me or someone else, it would start to affect and strain our relationship. We wouldn't be as close and as intimate as we could be. As we *want* to be. It would hurt him.

That's how Jesus feels. He so longs to be intimate with us, to live in a close, loving, divine romance with us. And when we make decisions that hurt us or hurt others, it hurts Him. It puts up a wall between Him and us. He doesn't put up the wall; our sin does. He is holy, and we are to be holy even as He is holy.

> " Grace doesn't give us license to sin; it actually empowers us to live rightly. "

In the book of Esther, Esther prepares for her union with the king by spending a year being "purified." She is set apart *before* the wedding. We are preparing for a wedding with our Bridegroom. When He comes, He will set all things right. But as we prepare for His arrival, we should be like Esther, cleansing and purifying and readying ourselves for our union with Him.

Holiness involves turning from our sin, repenting, and receiving forgiveness as well as serving Him and worshiping Him. If we truly want to see revival, we can't forget these things. We can't say we've moved past them. Grace doesn't give us license to sin; it actually empowers us to live rightly.

Be Transformed

What does this look like? Romans 12:2 says, *"Do not be conformed to this world, but be transformed by the renewal of your mind, that by testing you may discern what is the will of God, what is good and acceptable and perfect"* (ESV). Don't be conformed to the world. Don't do what the world does. Renew your mind in the presence of Jesus. Let God tell you what is good and acceptable and perfect—and what isn't.

When He shows you something that isn't good or acceptable or perfect, get it out. Get rid of it. Don't wait a single minute. There's nothing we could hang on to that would be better than closeness with Jesus. Don't let a single thing get in the way of what God wants to do in you and through you.

> " He loves to cleanse us and purify us from all unrighteousness and bring us even closer to Him. "

I have such good news for you. If there are things in your life that need to get out, He will take them. You can lay them down, right now, and He will take them for you. He is a good Daddy. He loves to cleanse us and purify us from all unrighteousness and bring us even closer to Him.

Heavenly Father, thank You that You have been so full of grace for me that You have forgiven me of so many things. Lord, I repent if I have taken Your

143

grace for granted, if I have used it and done my own thing. Lord, I repent of every sin, of everything that is not of You, of everything that I have put in front of You. I repent of every idol, whether it is ministry, jobs, or whatever.

[Take a minute here and confess whatever God shows you. What is in your heart that is not of Him? First John 1:9 says, *"If we confess our sins, He is faithful and just to forgive us our sins and to cleanse us from all unrighteousness."* All unrighteousness. Every single bit.]

I put You first, Jesus. I want You first in my life. I want to have eyes for only You. Jesus, will You put Holy Spirit blinders on my eyes so that I would only see You? Put blinders on what I watch on TV, or in the movie cinemas, or in my reading materials. Lord, convict my heart of anything that grieves Your Spirit.

Lord, I want to be a pure vessel for You to anoint, for You to use in this next coming outpouring. Jesus, You paid such a high price for me, and I thank You for that.

Lord, I take authority over every sin in my life—everything I did and shouldn't have done and everything I didn't do that I should have. I bring it to the foot of the cross, and God, I ask You to forgive me.

Lord, I want to be pure. Help me be pure. I don't want it to be an outward striving or a performance. Lord, I want it to be a passionate love affair with

You. Lord, would You give me a passionate love
for You? Give me an unquenchable love.

Just you watch Him do it. He will purify and cleanse you, and He will pour into you a passion for Him that others will look at and say, "I want to be like that." Oh, church, let's ask Him to ignite a fiery passion for Jesus that can never be quenched. Let's go into all the world and set it on fire.

NOTES

1. Wright, *Waves of Revival*, 23.
2. Ibid.

Chapter 10

The Stewardship

And they continued steadfastly in the apostles'
doctrine and fellowship, in the breaking of bread,
and in prayers. Then fear came upon every soul,
and many wonders and signs were done through
the apostles. Now all who believed were together,
and had all things in common, and sold their
possessions and goods, and divided them among
all, as anyone had need.

So continuing daily with one accord in the temple,
and breaking bread from house to house, they ate
their food with gladness and simplicity of heart,
praising God and having favor with all the people.
And the Lord added to the church daily those who
were being saved.

—ACTS 2:42-47

IN THE BOOK OF ACTS, THE HOLY SPIRIT FELL POWERFULLY—IN
chapter 2. There are 26 more chapters in Acts that record what
happened next.

What happens after a revival such as what broke out in Toronto in 1994? Even more pressing, what will happen after the next wave breaks over us? Even though God seems to break in upon us suddenly and we don't know the hour or the day, it's important that we prepare for it. We must steward the revival, the presence.

What does it mean to "steward" something? The word means, in this sense, "to manage or look after another's property." We are to "look after" the presence of the Holy Spirit. Throughout church history, there are examples of revivals that began powerfully, then fizzled out—not because the Holy Spirit didn't do what He was supposed to, but because people didn't steward the outpouring well. Scripture is very clear that we are to look after what God has given us.

> " Even though God seems to break in upon us suddenly and we don't know the hour or the day, it's important that we prepare for it. We must steward the revival, the presence. "

The Parable of the Talents

Matthew 25 is a very familiar story about stewardship. We've often made it about money, and it is about money. But God has given us many resources and gifts, and it's important that we understand stewardship as a big-picture principle.

> *For the kingdom of heaven is like a man traveling to a far country, who called his own servants and*

delivered his goods to them. And to one he gave five talents, to another two, and to another one, to each according to his own ability; and immediately he went on a journey. Then he who had received the five talents went and traded with them, and made another five talents. And likewise he who had received two gained two more also. But he who had received one went and dug in the ground, and hid his lord's money (Matthew 25:14-18).

Here we have three men, each given a measure of the master's wealth to steward. The first two men went out and multiplied what the master had given them, but the third buried it. He hid it. And what happened when the master came back?

After a long time the lord of those servants came and settled accounts with them. So he who had received five talents came and brought five other talents, saying, "Lord, you delivered to me five talents; look, I have gained five more talents besides them." His lord said to him, "Well done, good and faithful servant; you were faithful over a few things, I will make you ruler over many things. Enter into the joy of your lord." He also who had received two talents came and said, "Lord, you delivered to me two talents; look, I have gained two more talents besides them." His lord said to him, "Well done, good and faithful servant; you have been faithful over a few things, I will make you ruler over many things. Enter into the joy of your lord" (Matthew 25:19-23).

The first two men who stewarded the gifts well were invited into the joy of the Lord. They were made rulers over many things. Those men took the master's gifts out in to the community. They did business and multiplied the gifts. Well done indeed. But the third man:

> *Then he who had received the one talent came and said, "Lord, I knew you to be a hard man, reaping where you have not sown, and gathering where you have not scattered seed. And I was afraid, and went and hid your talent in the ground. Look, there you have what is yours."*
>
> *But his lord answered and said to him, "You wicked and lazy servant, you knew that I reap where I have not sown, and gather where I have not scattered seed. So you ought to have deposited my money with the bankers, and at my coming I would have received back my own with interest. Therefore take the talent from him, and give it to him who has ten talents"* (Matthew 25:24-28).

The third man finds himself not only without an increase but without the gifts altogether. What little he had was taken away from him and given to the ones who had done well. Some have read this parable to mean that God keeps giving to the wealthy and takes away from the poor. But that's not the point at all. You see, it wasn't that the third servant did anything wrong; the problem was that he did nothing.

We are not given the gifts of God to hide them away. We are given those gifts so we can multiply them and give even more away. And if this is true about money, how much more is it true about the presence of the Holy Spirit?

Two Kinds of Stewardship

There are two ways we need to steward the presence. One, our personal lives should reflect the change in our worldview that has come from our experience with the Holy Spirit. And two, there is a corporate stewardship where our church families reflect the same experience.

Personal Stewardship

When the Holy Spirit comes upon us and radically shifts our hearts and minds, it is crucial that we as individuals steward this shift. It's like falling in love; if I want my relationship with the person I'm in love with to be good, there are some things I need to do. Now the good news is, when I'm in love I *want* to do those things.

One of the most important ways to steward what God has done in us personally is through soaking. In the early days when we would talk about soaking, people got really rattled. They said it sounded "weird." Just sitting there, or lying there, not doing anything? How can that be good? It sounded "New Age-y," some of the critics said, like transcendental meditation

> "When the Holy Spirit comes upon us and radically shifts our hearts and minds, it is crucial that we as individuals steward this shift."

or something. But this is very different from that method of meditation, which asks you to empty your mind and just let whatever come in and take over.

That's not soaking at all. When I soak, I focus on my beloved, on my Jesus. I focus on His character, on His presence, on His love. He has shown me His face, and I gaze into His eyes as I soak. I am never "empty." I am full because I am falling deeper and deeper in love with Him.

When I'm falling in love, I want to be in the presence of the person I love. It doesn't matter what we do; it's just important that we are together. When the Holy Spirit has come upon you and turned your heart toward Jesus, His intention is that it wouldn't be a one-time thing. His intention is that the love that got stirred up during your encounter would continue every day. When we fall down in a meeting, it's not the falling down that's the important part. It's the staying down, marinating in His presence. When you have a love affair, it's not a five-minute fling. A love affair takes time.

Soaking

"Marinating" is a really good way to describe soaking. When I am going to grill a good steak, I will often marinate it before I cook it. Marinating is an interesting process. The contents of the marinade get all down into the fibers of the meat, and once that meat has been marinated you can never separate the two things again. That meat will never be un-marinated. That's why we soak—marinate—in God's presence. We want every bit of us to be soaked in Him so that we can never be un-soaked. We can never go back to the way we were before.

The meat only had to do one thing—just be in the presence of that marinade. I love worship (we'll talk more about it in this chapter). I love prayer. I love to talk to Jesus, to pour out my heart to Him. But sometimes the Lord just wants me to come and be with Him, without an agenda.

How do we soak? What does that look like? Well, first, it looks like getting still. Psalm 46:10 says, "Be busy and know that I am God."

Right?

No, of course not. That's not what it says at all. The verse actually says, *"Be still, and know that I am God."* Do you know how to be still? It's hard. We have been trained since the time we were little children to go, go, go. Be Marthas, be Marthas, be Marthas. Our schoolteachers, our parents, our pastors never taught us to be still. We need to get still so that He—not me—can tell you that He is your God. That He is the One who loves you. That He is the one who will always be there, that He will never leave you or forsake you.

> We need to get still so that He—not me—can tell you that He is your God. That He is the One who loves you. That He is the One who will always be there, that He will never leave you or forsake you.

Soaking is simply resting before Him, coming into a place of peace. This takes practice; we have very busy minds and very busy lives, and it takes some practice to learn to get quiet. I like to lie down somewhere comfortable, maybe on the floor with a pillow under my head or on a couch. I have soaked sitting up in a comfortable chair too, but if you sit in a chair be sure to sit in such a way that you don't have to think about your position. (Don't cross your legs; you may not realize it, but that's not going to be a comfortable position for a long time. You're going to need to shift a lot if you sit that way. It's better to sit with your legs down, if you choose to sit.)

Get comfortable. Then begin to listen. Tune in to God. You have control over your mind, and you can choose what you focus on. So tune in to the voice of God. The enemy sometimes has a loud voice, and our own thoughts can be pretty loud too. But God's voice is that still, small voice. Unless we tune our hearts in to Him, we can sometimes miss Him.

We want to learn to experience the reality of God, not just in a conference or in a meeting but in your own room. In your own living room. In your own car. Wherever you are. You can experience His presence anywhere you are, not just at church. You can take that few minutes and say, "Oh Lord, I just position myself to be with You," even if it's just for a few minutes.

I usually have a little notebook or something right by me when I soak. At first, there are a thousand things running through my head. Some of them are the enemy, and some of them come from my own brain. So I just write them all down. "Thank you for reminding me. I'll write it down so I don't forget." Eventually, the enemy realizes he's not going to distract me, and I go back to soaking.

And then, I just rest. I rest in His presence, listening to His voice, enjoying the pictures and impressions He gives me. After the Holy Spirit fell in 1994, I learned to soak in His presence and I kept my end of the love affair going and going and going and going. It still hasn't stopped. I know He will never stop loving me and pursuing me and wanting to spend time with me, so I purposely cultivate these intimate times with Him. Soaking is intentionally getting into the presence of God by faith, and just being with Him. Through soaking, I've been transformed.

Worship

Like soaking, worship places us in God's presence. Anything that puts you in the middle of God's presence is a good thing. But unlike soaking, we are very active when we worship.

Most of us think of worship as what happens at church with a band and a sound system and music and words on the screen. And that is definitely an important thing, and we should worship together with our church family. But worship isn't about music or musicians or words. It's about expressing our love for God and His absolute holiness and worthiness. And we can do that with or without a guitar.

The Psalms are a great place to learn about worship. Read them out loud. And when you do sing, remember that in Psalm 100 David said we should make a joyful noise to the Lord.

> It's about expressing our love for God and His absolute holiness and worthiness. And we can do that with or without a guitar.

Church

In Acts 2, after the Holy Spirit fell on the believers and 3,000 more were added they had a church. A real live church, full of people who needed to know how to steward what had happened in the Upper Room and how they should live now.

Acts says that *"all who believed were together, and had all things in common...continuing daily with one accord"* (Acts 2:44,46). They gathered together to pray, to worship, to learn, and to continue to grow in the Lord and in the things of the Spirit.

Part of personally stewarding the gift of the Holy Spirit that was poured out on you is gathering together with other believers. It's putting yourself in environments that welcome the work of the Holy Spirit and allowing others to impart to you. Find a church that embraces the presence and power of the Holy Spirit and gather with the other believers there.

Corporate Stewardship

Gathering with other believers in the context of church lets us corporately steward the coming revival. There are a couple of ways we can do that.

Worship

Like private worship, worshiping together with other believers proclaiming our love for God and His majesty and holiness places us right in the center of His presence. It so stirs our hearts to worship together. At Catch the Fire in Toronto, we have an amazing group of musicians who lead us right into the throne room. What a blessing. And I know that at churches all over the world, men and women are using

> As we host the presence as a church body, we make room for the power and the presence of the Holy Spirit to move on us again and again and again and again.

their God-given talents and abilities to lead their congregations in worship.

Spending time together in worship allows us to welcome the Holy Spirit to continue to move among us, for healing to break out, for encouraging prophetic words to be spoken, for the captives to be set free—right in our meetings. As we host the presence as a church body, we make room for the power and the presence of the Holy Spirit to move on us again and again and again and again.

Intentionality

Stewarding the presence takes being intentional. It means setting some good things aside in order to prioritize the best thing. It means beginning to live a life of personal revival now, preparing to host the massive wave that's coming. Soaking, worshiping, consuming the Word, gathering with other revival-seeking believers—all of these things are crucial to keeping our hearts ready.

Consequences of Revival

Throughout revival history, when the Holy Spirit came upon people many things happened. Initially, what we would call "manifestations of the Spirit" would happen—laughing, shaking, falling down, tears, etc. All of these are very common, starting with the book of Acts and continuing until today. This is very exciting to be a part of. People being consumed with joy, being electrified by God—it's fun to see and experience.

Repentance

But there is so much more that happens when the Holy Spirit shows up in power. We've already talked about how it creates such an intimacy with God, how it draws us deep into a divine love affair with God. When the Holy Spirit showed up in the book of Acts, one of the very first things that happened was mass repentance. In Acts 2:38, Peter says, *"Repent, and let every one of you be baptized in the name of Jesus Christ for the remission of sins; and you shall receive the gift of the Holy Spirit."* Then a bit later in verse 40, he says, *"Be saved from this perverse generation."* And they did. Verse 41 says that they *"gladly received his word."* Revival leads to repentance.

> Revival leads to repentance.

This is going to be a holiness revival. Those inside and outside the church are going to be convicted by the Holy Spirit and are going to run to the cross for forgiveness. Are we ready for it? Are we ready for the "3,000" who will run to us, looking for the truth?

Growth

Living things grow. Where there is Holy Spirit life, things will grow. And when there is revival happening, you will see the churches growing exponentially. This is a good thing, but we need to know just what it is we're asking for.

When the Holy Spirit fell in 1994, we ended up having meetings six nights a week. People began streaming through our doors by the hundreds and then the thousands—which quickly became hard for our staff and leaders. We began to rotate them in and out, giving them nights off. Our church grew as a result of the outpouring, and we began to train up volunteers and leaders to help. Be frank with your leaders now, as you prepare for the big wave. Although we don't know exactly how this next move will look, we know that it will cost something. Let's all be ready.

The good news is, as we fall more and more deeply in love, we serve Him not because we are slaves but because we are sons and daughters who love their heavenly Father and who love people and desperately want to see the earth filled with His glory.

> *We are sons and daughters who love their heavenly Father and who love people and desperately want to see the earth filled with His glory.*

Influence

After January 20, 1994, our little church was thrust into the spotlight. We suddenly had influence we'd never had before, and it was a little overwhelming sometimes. But when God begins to pour out miracles and healings and freedom, the world is going to get wind of it. They're going to be talking about it. They're going to want to come and see for themselves what's going on. They're going to come in our doors from all over the world, just like they did then. And they're going to look to us for answers: What is happening here? What is God doing? Why is that person doing that? We are the ones they will ask.

It's so important that we remember that although we are vessels chosen by God, we are just that—vessels. The ultimate goal is not that we would be made famous, but that the name of Jesus Christ would be made famous in all the earth. We need to steward our influence from a place of humility and love instead of wealth and power. Remember, we were once outside the family too. It took the love of Jesus and some crazy revival-minded people to love us into the Kingdom.

The Outward Journey

This is part of the outward journey we talked about in Chapter 4. Revival isn't just for the church; it's for the whole world. It's not so we can say, "Us four and no more." It's so we can invite a very lost and very hurting world to a wedding feast.

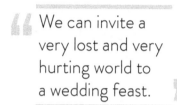

> We can invite a very lost and very hurting world to a wedding feast.

Consequences in the Church

Revival isn't just for the lost. It definitely is for the lost; God displays His mighty power and His beautiful sacrificial love for those outside the Kingdom. But it's also for those of us already in the church. It like Holy Spirit brings His defibrillator to wake us up, to jumpstart our hearts too. We get revitalized, reawakened to His presence.

Unity

In Ephesians 4, Paul is instructing the Ephesians how to live after they've received the Holy Spirit. In verse 1, he says, "*I, therefore, the prisoner of the Lord, beseech you to walk worthy of the calling with which you were called, with all lowliness and gentleness, with longsuffering, bearing with one another in love, endeavoring to keep the unity of the Spirit in the bond of peace*" (Eph. 4:1-3). Because the Holy Spirit has now come upon us, we are to bear with one another in love and work for unity in the Spirit.

Unity here means "oneness." We are one family, bonded in the Spirit and what He's done in us. But that doesn't mean we all look the same. If you were to meet everyone who has come through our doors in the past 20-plus years, you would find a wide variety of nationalities, skin colors, dress preferences, music preferences, etc. The goal of revival is not to make clones. It's to make a family. And families are full of people who are different from one another.

So if we are different, how do we "bear with one another"? We learn how to confront when we've been hurt. We learn how to repent to one another when we've made mistakes. We don't sweep things under the rug. Instead, we learn how to do relationships well. Earlier in the book of Ephesians, Paul talks about how the *"manifold wisdom of God might be made known by the church to the principalities and powers in the heavenly places"* (Eph. 3:10). How do we make the manifold wisdom of God known to the principalities and powers? According to Paul, it's by doing relationships well. It's by loving well. It's by continually learning how to love each other well.

> Families are full of people who are different from one another.

There was an old song that went like this: "They will know we are Christians by our love." The world will see what God is doing when we love people well.

Healing

One of the major outcomes of what happened in Toronto in 1994 was massive healings that took place. Tumors disappeared, limbs grew out, and many serious back and neck injuries were healed. And those who were touched by the revival saw healing break out in their own ministry.

Many will know that Heidi and Rolland Baker visited us in Toronto in 1997. Up to that point, the Bakers had been missionaries in Hong Kong, Indonesia, and Mozambique but were now burned out and exhausted. Rolland came to Toronto first and was wonderfully refreshed. Then Heidi came and had a powerful encounter with the Holy Spirit that left her under the power and unable to function for several days. When they returned to Mozambique, everything changed.

> After she returned to the mission field in Mozambique she began praying for the blind but not getting good results. Until about a year later, when a blind beggar lady came to church. Heidi was thrilled to pray for her because she wasn't going to give up on the word that she had received from the Lord. As she prayed for the lady, her eyes began to turn from white to gray and then to brown. The next day she prayed for another woman who was blind since the age of eight. This lady received her sight too. On the third day, Heidi prayed for yet another woman who was blind from birth and she received her sight. All three of these women were named Mama Aida. In Mozambique, Heidi's name is also Mama Aida.[1]

Heidi has since seen countless healings and miracles and has planted thousands of churches in Africa. But you don't have to be a Heidi or a Rolland Baker to see healings. When the Holy Spirit comes on you, you are empowered to heal just like they are. And when the Holy Spirit comes on your church and your city, you will see healings like never before.

Get ready. The Spirit is about to pour out in a way the world has never seen before. This next wave will make the book of Acts look tame and controlled.

> When the Holy Spirit comes on your church and your city, you will see healings like never before.

If that's the case, we need to be ready to steward it, both personally and in our churches. We need to be prepared for the multitudes who will run to the cross and then run in our church doors. We need to think and plan and pray and intentionally pursue the holiness and the power and the presence of God *before* the wave hits.

We are preparing for the glory to fall. Because we haven't seen anything yet.

ACTIVATE

Spend some time soaking this week. Start with 15 minutes or so; I guarantee you will want to soak more! Get quiet, get alone with Him, and just rest there. Intentionally, by faith, rest in His anointing and presence. You'll be amazed at how close He is and how intimate He is. Just rest and enjoy Him!

NOTE

1. Christy Biswell, "Heidi Baker: Intimacy for Miracles," CBN.com, September 17, 2013, http://www1.cbn.com/700club/heidi-baker-intimacy-miracles.

Chapter 11

The Promise

And while staying with them he ordered them not to depart from Jerusalem, but to wait for the promise of the Father, which, he said, "you heard from me; for John baptized with water, but you will be baptized with the Holy Spirit not many days from now."

—Acts 1:4-5 ESV

Can you imagine being one of the 120 in the Upper Room? Jesus has been arrested, tried, crucified—and now resurrected. People you know have seen Him! Some of the disciples talked about the day He went up to Heaven in a cloud, and the two men (angels? Someone said they might be angels) came and spoke to the disciples.

It's a strange time, in some ways. This little band of people who believe Jesus was who He said He was are learning how to commit their lives to living as He did. You get together with them sometimes, and you pray and talk about all the things you saw Him do and all the things He said. Miracles! Healing! And the way He loved His friends—well, no one had ever seen that before. You miss Him. You all do.

He had made some promises before He left. Or rather, He had told you that His Father had made some promises, and He had to go away so that the Father could fulfill those promises. What were they, again?

Oh, yes, the Holy Spirit! You're not sure exactly what that means, but if Jesus said it and the Father promised it, it must be good.

The Glory

What might the disciples have expected when they gathered that day? Remember, most of these people would not have been educated by that culture's standards, and they may or may not have known the theology behind who the Holy Spirit was. What context would they have had for what was about to happen?

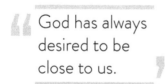
God has always desired to be close to us.

In the book of Exodus, Moses asked God to show him His glory, but God told him that no one could look upon Him and live. So God hid Moses in the cleft of the rock because to show Moses His full glory would have killed him. The word for "glory" in that passage is the word *kābōd*, which means wealth or honor or majesty, from a root meaning weight or heavy.. Jesus's followers would be very familiar with that story.

They would also have known the story of Israel wandering in the desert, following the cloud by day and the pillar of fire by night. Those signs were physical manifestations of the presence of God in the Tent of Meeting in the desert. It was the presence of His glory.

The Presence

Exodus 25 describes a very exact listing of the furniture that is to go in the Tent of Meeting and later into the Temple, including a description of the Table of Showbread.

> *You shall make a table of acacia wood. Two cubits shall be its length, a cubit its breadth, and a cubit and a half its height. You shall overlay it with pure gold and make a molding of gold around it. And you shall make a rim around it a handbreadth wide, and a molding of gold around the rim. And you shall make for it four rings of gold, and fasten the rings to the four corners at its four legs. Close to the frame the rings shall lie, as holders for the poles to carry the table. You shall make the poles of acacia wood, and overlay them with gold, and the table shall be carried with these. And you shall make its plates and dishes for incense, and its flagons and bowls with which to pour drink offerings; you shall make them of pure gold. **And you shall set the bread of the Presence on the table before me regularly** (Exodus 25:23-30 ESV).*

The Bread of the Presence! God has always desired to be close to us. Even there in the Temple, well before Jesus arrived on the scene, God was providing ways to experience His presence. The disciples would have been very familiar with the Temple. Most of them had spent their lives following Temple traditions, and the emphasis on the presence of God would not have been a foreign concept at all.

Other Old Testament References

Joshua was filled with the "spirit of wisdom" after Moses laid hands on him (see Deut. 34:9). Elijah and Elisha were both filled with the Spirit of the Lord (see 2 Kings 2:9,15). The book of Ezekiel is filled with references to the "Spirit of the Lord."

The disciples also would have been very familiar with Isaiah 61:1: *"The Spirit of the Lord God is upon Me, because the Lord has anointed Me."* They had heard Jesus quote this very verse—about Himself.

Fire

If you had been a Hebrew during Jesus's time, you would have been familiar with the Old Testament stories where God showed up in fire. For example, the first time God spoke to Moses it was in a burning bush. When He led the Israelites in the desert it was with a pillar of fire by night.

Ezekiel 1:4 describes the approaching glory of the Lord: *"As I looked, behold, a stormy wind came out of the north, and a great cloud, with brightness around it, and fire flashing forth continually, and in the midst of the fire, as it were gleaming metal"* (ESV).

Wind

In Hebrew, the word for the Holy Spirit is *rûaḥ ha qodesh*. The words mean "holy breath, wind, or spirit." They describe what God does—breathes, blows, and moves through the wind. In other words, God sends and works through the wind, most commonly the *rûaḥ*.

Isaiah 32 uses that word in a different way, though: *"Until the Spirit [rûaḥ] is poured upon us from on high, and the wilderness becomes a fruitful field, and the fruitful field is counted as a forest"* (Isa. 32:15). When the "wind" is poured upon us from on high, everything will change. The whole landscape will look different, and there will be life.

Breath

Similar to "wind" is the idea of God breathing on us. In Genesis 3, God formed Adam from the dust of the ground and then "breathed" life into Him.

In Ezekiel 37, the Spirit takes the prophet to a valley where there are dry bones just lying around. This is what the Spirit tells the prophet:

> *Again He said to me, "Prophesy to these bones, and say to them, 'O dry bones, hear the word of the Lord! Thus says the Lord God to these bones: "Surely I will cause breath to enter into you, and you shall live. I will put sinews on you and bring flesh upon you, cover you with skin and put breath in you; and you shall live. Then you shall know that I am the Lord."'" So I prophesied as I was commanded; and as I prophesied, there was a noise, and suddenly a rattling; and the bones*

came together, bone to bone. Indeed, as I looked, the sinews and the flesh came upon them, and the skin covered them over; but there was no breath in them. Also He said to me, "Prophesy to the breath, prophesy, son of man, and say to the breath, 'Thus says the Lord God: "Come from the four winds, O breath, and breathe on these slain, that they may live."'" So I prophesied as He commanded me, and breath came into them, and they lived, and stood upon their feet, an exceedingly great army (Ezekiel 37:4-10).

God breathed on what was clearly dead—and it came to life again. They lived and stood on their feet, an exceedingly great army. What a picture of revival, of the Spirit sweeping into the room on the breath of God!

After Jesus was resurrected, there are several places where He visits the disciples. On one of these visits, John 20:22 relates how Jesus breathed on the disciples. He told them to receive the Holy Spirit; some scholars believe the Upper Room experience may have started right then and there.

> Command the dead things to live. Invite God to breathe on you! Go ahead.

Why don't you stop right now and prophesy to the bones? Command the dead things to live. Invite God to breathe on you! Go ahead.

You see, although the disciples wouldn't have had any idea about the Trinity or about the Holy Spirit as a person, they would be somewhat familiar with the ways He might show up.

Jesus and the Spirit

Throughout Jesus's ministry, His followers saw the Holy Spirit at work through Jesus. Many of them would have watched the dove descend after John baptized Him, even though they may not have known exactly what it meant. The followers with Him that day may have heard the voice from Heaven and God talking about His Son.

Then they would have seen the miracles. Leprosy healed. Tumors healed. Blind eyes opened. I think sometimes we read these accounts like they're nice little healings with no drama or Holy Spirit attached. But I think every time Jesus performed a

> Jesus never did the same thing the same way twice.

miracle, the presence and power of the Spirit was totally evident. They were dramatic enough to attract the attention of the Pharisees, after all. I also suspect Jesus Himself just carried such a thick anointing that it was hard to miss.

We mentioned that Jesus had quoted Isaiah 61 about Himself, so the disciples knew firsthand what it looked like when someone was filled with the Spirit of God. They knew what the power and the presence looked like.

The Anticipation

As the disciples gathered in the Upper Room, all of these images would have been in their minds. They would have discussed it with each other, reminding each other of all the instances they knew about. "Remember when Jesus did this or that?"

"Oh, yes! And remember when that man got healed? Goosebumps!"

"What do you think about the way He blew on us? Something definitely happened to me! I wonder if this will be like that."

"God talked to Moses in a burning bush. *A burning bush.* Like, it was on fire!"

"I know, man. So crazy! I wonder what will happen this time."

They knew something was about to happen. As they gathered to wait, the anticipation began to build. Although they had some picture of how things might be, they knew better than to put God in a box. After all, they'd been with Jesus for over three years. He never did the same thing the same way twice.

The Waiting

In John 14, Jesus tells His disciples the plan. "I'm going away," He says, "to prepare a place for you with My Father. By the way, I'm the way to get to the Father! If you know Me, you know Him!" In verse 9, He says:

> *Have I been with you so long, and yet you have not known Me, Philip? He who has seen Me has seen the Father; so how can you say, "Show us the Father"? Do you not believe that I am in the Father, and the Father in Me? The words that I speak to*

you I do not speak on My own authority; but the Father who dwells in Me does the works. Believe Me that I am in the Father and the Father in Me, or else believe Me for the sake of the works themselves (John 14:9-11).

What a statement. "If you've seen Me, you've seen the Father." So what kind of Father had the disciples seen? Well, if He was like Jesus, and Jesus said He was, then the Father was kind and generous and loving and powerful and good and just and.... That was the Father who had made a promise. A good, loving Father.

> As they were waiting for this unknown event, they could rest in the idea that it was coming from a Father they could trust.

As they were waiting for this unknown event, they could rest in the idea that it was coming from a Father they could trust.

The Promise

Most assuredly, I say to you, he who believes in Me, the works that I do he will do also; and greater works than these he will do, because I go to My Father. And whatever you ask in My name, that I will do, that the Father may be glorified in the Son. If you ask anything in My name, I will do it.

If you love Me, keep My commandments. And I will pray the Father, and He will give you another Helper, that He may abide with you forever—the

Spirit of truth, whom the world cannot receive, because it neither sees Him nor knows Him; but you know Him, for He dwells with you and will be in you. I will not leave you orphans; I will come to you (John 14:12-18).

Jesus makes a similar statement in Acts 1, calling it the "promise of the Father." The Father would give them a Helper—the Spirit of truth. This good Father whom they could trust, through Jesus whom they knew intimately, had made them a promise. Whatever was coming, it was going to be good!

The Promise Fulfilled

So there you are, waiting with your friends and family in the Upper Room. The air is thick with the anticipation, whispered reminders of the promise between you. Your stomach is in knots; when will it happen? Will it be today?

Then the air stills. Voices hush, without anyone giving instruction. Even the birds seem to stop their singing, and the chatter in the street fades.

Suddenly, a mighty wind sweeps through the room. You watch in amazement as it starts on one side and moves quickly through. As it touches various people, they begin to laugh. Some begin to weep. Every single person drops to the ground as if shot, where they shake and roll.

Then it hits you. Every nerve feels alive. It seems as if every cell in your body has been struck by lightning, and you begin to shake under the power. You watch in amazement as your hand moves at a speed you didn't know was possible. You can't imagine what it looks like to everyone else...and then you realize that no one is paying a bit of attention to you because they are all having a similar experience.

Something begins to bubble up in your belly. You're not quite sure what it is; should you let it out? It's a new sensation. You've never felt this before. But something in your mind says, "Well, why not?" and you let it out.

From deep within you, laughter begins to erupt. You feel it burst out of you, and you wonder if it's like the lightning you felt a minute ago. This laughter is like nothing you've ever felt before. It seems to seep from your belly outward to your feet, your arms, and your face. Your cheeks begin to hurt from the intensity, but you realize you never want it to stop.

You try to stand up, but you realize that might be difficult—which makes you laugh even harder. Your head feels deliciously light, almost as if you've had too much wine; but there's no headache, no confusion. Only more clarity than you've ever known.

The laughter subsides for just a minute, and you stop to look around the room. Just to your left, one of your friends is pointing at your head in amazement, just as you begin to point at his head in amazement.

There, hovering just above his head, is *fire.* Not a little fire—a dancing tongue of fire. You reach up over your head— *ow!* It's real fire. You look back at your friend with his tongue of fire, and you both begin to laugh again.

So this is what Jesus was talking about, you think. *This must be the Holy Spirit!* Wind. Fire. Familiar descriptions of God showing up. *He is here,* you think. And once again you fall to the floor, that sweet laughter overtaking you again.

This is joy. This is...it's love, you realize. Overwhelming, tangible love has just overtaken your entire being, and you know you will never get enough.

As We Wait

We are in a similar situation as the disciples, aren't we? Of course we have a bit of an advantage; the Holy Spirit is now being poured out on all flesh. We have full access to everything Jesus promised, even as we wait for what's next.

> " The earth will be filled with the knowledge of the glory of the Lord as the waters cover the sea. "

We also have the advantage of looking to history for what to expect. Revival history is full of the glory and power of the Holy Spirit on display. Even just looking back to 1994, we have some idea of what God wants to do.

And we know what a good Father we have. We know intimately how He wants to heal our hearts, how He wants to be so intimate with us. We know how He wants to be our first priority because He's in love with us. We know He has invited us to a wedding, and He is preparing us for it.

We know He has promised us a bigger wave, an outpouring that will dwarf what we've seen before. We know that it will be an outpouring that will produce holiness and a return to God. But we don't know exactly what that will look like, do we?

Expectant

It's easy to put God in a box, isn't it? It would be easy to say, "Well, we know how God has done it before, so He'll do it the same way again." We like what we know. We like our comfort zones.

When the Holy Spirit fell in 1994, there were some familiar things about it—the laughter, the falling down, the healings, and the speaking in tongues. All of these manifestations are recorded throughout revival history. But what we didn't see coming were the thousands and thousands of people who would come and who would be introduced to a Father who wanted to heal

> " We know what a good Father we have. We know intimately how He wants to heal our hearts. "

their hearts. We didn't know that it would spread like wildfire to America, to England, to Africa, to Australia, and around the world. We didn't know that 20-plus years later, we would be planting churches in all of those places that would spread this revival. In fact, we didn't know the revival would still be going after 20-plus years.

What we did know was that we wanted God to move. We knew that He had promised us that He would. We knew that He is a good Father, and that He keeps His promises. Beyond that, we just knew we wanted more.

In the Waiting

We are waiting again. We are expecting again. God has made promises to us again, and this time He says it will be bigger than the world has ever seen before. We are waiting for the promise of the Father, just like the disciples were.

I want to encourage you to wait like they did. Look to what you know as signposts—God will show up in ways that you will recognize are God. Just like the disciples felt that wind and saw that fire and knew that it was God, so we will see signs of God moving. He will once again pour out His Spirit on all flesh, releasing His love and joy and peace and righteousness. The earth will be filled with the knowledge of the glory of the Lord as the waters cover the sea.

It will happen. Let's get ready. Meet me in the Upper Room.

ACTIVATE

*Lord, we wait. We tarry. We expect You to move. And we position ourselves to see it when it happens! God, we wait like the disciples did in the Upper Room. We know how You've moved before—and we want more! We want more of Your Holy Spirit manifest on the earth. We want more healings, more deliverance, more joy, more peace— we want so much more of You! God, today we claim the promise that the earth **will** be filled with the knowledge of the glory of the Lord just like the waters cover the sea. Come, Holy Spirit, and move like You did in Acts. Come move like You did with John Wesley. Come move like You did in the revivals of history. Come move like you did in Toronto in 1994. Come, Holy Spirit, and move in ways we haven't seen yet! Come surprise us with Your sud- denlies. Come move mightily among us, and come move in the world around us. We love You, Holy Spirit! Come! More, Lord!*

Conclusion

THE NEXT WAVE OF REVIVAL IS BEING CALLED A "TSUNAMI," A BIGGER wave than we've ever seen.

A tsunami is an enormous wave, gigantic and powerful. Tsunamis begin in a region at the bottom of the ocean called the "Ring of Fire," where tectonic plates and volcanic activity are constantly in motion, shifting and firing and erupting—and causing earthquakes that cause massive waves at the surface.

Scientists can somewhat predict when and where a tsunami will hit. There are signs that begin at the bottom of the ocean—rumblings and shakings and quakings. They often will send out alarms and warnings to the people in the way of the wave.

People feel it, even if they don't always know what they're feeling. When those precursors become evident, preparations need to be made. Those in the path of the tsunami need to get ready. They may need to change location. They may need to change their living situation. They need to prepare.

The rumblings are happening. All over the world, the evidence that God is on the move is growing. The underground church in places like China and Iran is exploding. Muslims are reporting that Jesus is appearing to them—in their homes. In remote areas of Africa, villages who have never seen anyone from outside are being evangelized, learning the truth of Jesus Christ. Europe is undergoing massive change in its governments, as is America. The shaking is happening.

We quoted a prophetic word from Cindy Jacobs at the very beginning of this book that was given to us in January of 2014. The rest of her word says, "England is next, and then My Spirit will jump to Asia and the Pacific Rim. Europe will be ablaze with My glory and France will be touched in a glorious way. Not one continent will be left out, for this is a season when the anointing will fall on those who have come, both young and old, and they will go home rejoicing and carrying revival fire!"

> We may need to change how we do life.

Do you feel it?

Revivals can be compared to tsunamis. Earthquakes begin in Heaven, where God is in motion. He is constantly moving toward the day when Heaven and earth will be one, when the Bride and the Bridegroom will be joined in the Marriage Supper of the Lamb. He is always shaking up the way things are to bring them into alignment with the way they should be.

He is always shifting the landscape.

When a tsunami makes land, it sweeps away everything in its path. What stood in its way is reduced to rubble. Ways of life need to be rebuilt from the bottom up. Cities and governments often need to be restructured.

Our landscape is about to change. The tsunami wave of revival that will usher in the coming of the Lord is about to make land. The rumblings are evident; the evidence is clear. We are feeling the quaking. But though we would move away from a tsunami in the ocean, we run toward the tsunami of Heaven. We prepare, we take action, to be ready for the changes to come.

We may need to change how we do life. We may need to shift our priorities, change our focus. And we need to sound the alarm: "The Bridegroom is coming! The Bride is making herself ready!" The Marriage Supper of the Lamb is being prepared, and all are invited. The glory of the Lord is about to cover the earth like the waters cover the sea.

Are you ready?

Afterword

Randy Clark

I BELIEVE WHAT GOD RELEASED IN TORONTO BACK IN 1994 WAS not an isolated event; it was part of a great River of the Spirit that had been flowing in other parts of the world; and I also believe that this outpouring continues to this day.

As we prepare for what God is going to do next, I thought the following segment from my book, *Baptized in the Spirit*, would be a fitting way to close this most timely work by John and Carol Arnott. After all, their book could have easily been a memorial to the past, celebrating the "glory days" of Toronto. And there is much to celebrate about that wonderful move of God! But they didn't provide such a volume.

Preparing for the Glory, in my opinion, is an eschatological perspective on revival. Often, some expressions of eschatology (end-times theology) involve preparing believers for something

185

that's to come. In many popularized, bestselling end-times' works, the focus has been on preparing for collapse, disaster, and the unfolding of a satanic agenda. Well, *Preparing for the Glory* is the same—but different.

This invitation calls the body of Christ to be ready, for sure, but to be ready for the fulfillment of a prophesied outpouring that God wants to release into all the earth. I'm convinced we have a biblical mandate to continue to pursue this great move of God until we see the fulfillment of Acts 2—*all flesh* experiencing the wonderful outpouring of the Holy Spirit.

So, everything John and Carol celebrate about what God *has done* in the past has implications for us today. The Arnotts prepared for a sovereign *suddenly* of God. Even though God is sovereign, and thus, His sovereignty motivates His "suddenly" visitations, as John wrote about, I believe the Arnotts call us to model the early church and give practical teaching on how to position ourselves for another great *suddenly* move of God.

We commit to being good stewards of what He is currently doing, while pressing in and positioning ourselves for new dimensions of the Spirit's outpouring.

Revival in the 1990s

The mid-1990s witnessed the beginnings of yet another revival. This particular move of God has been called by many names: Laughing Revival, Toronto Blessing, Brownsville Revival, and Smithton Awakening. It began in 1992 in Argentina with pastor Claudio Freidzon. Miracles, signs, and wonders broke out in his church, followed by explosive growth.

On the heels of this Holy Spirit fire in Argentina, "fire" broke out in Lakeland, Florida, at Karl Strader's church, the Carpenter's Home Church. This happened when evangelist Rodney Howard-Browne came to speak. People fell down under the power of God, oftentimes unable to get up for quite some time. Weeping and laughter also characterized this particular move of God. Many considered the laughter a new and novel manifestation when in fact laughter can be found during other outpourings, within both Protestant and Roman Catholic revival history.

Then in January 1994, revival broke out in Toronto, Canada, when I went to speak for a planned four-day meeting. I was the bridge between Howard-Browne and what happened in Toronto. I had gone to receive ministry from Rodney twice before going to Toronto. The outpouring of the Spirit happened in my church for months and at the regional meeting of the Vineyard in the Midwest when I spoke prior to going to Toronto. Those meetings were the reason John Arnott invited me to come to Toronto.

I had already experienced my suddenly, but it was to continue with even greater moving from hiddenness to a world platform. This revival in Toronto became the longest protracted meeting in Western history, with people gathering six nights a week for twelve-and-a-half years until the summer of 2006. The influence from Toronto quickly spread around the world. During the first two years, more than two million people came to Toronto for the meetings.

Some say as many as four million came during the first five years, and reports indicate over 50,000 churches were touched during the first three to four years. An army of itinerates who had been touched by God went out to preach the Good News. It would not be an exaggeration to believe that thousands went out to the nations.

The controversy over Toronto was great, just as it was during the First Great Awakening, the Second Great Awakening, the Holiness Revival, the Pentecostal Revival, the mid-20th-century Revival, the Charismatic Renewal, and the Third Wave Revival. However, I can testify to the authenticity of this move of God because He birthed it through me. I wrote the book *There Is More* to reveal the massive good fruit of this move and to provide a biblical and historical basis for the doctrine of laying on of hands (see Hebrews 6:1-2). Previous to this I had written a book called *Lighting Fires* that describes how this move came about.

It is impossible to know how many souls have come into the Kingdom as a result of God's touch in Toronto, but I do know with certainty that the testimony of three people in particular who were profoundly touched by God through the Toronto Blessing have been used to lead more than three million to the Lord. They are Henry Madava (Ukraine), Heidi Baker (Mozambique), and Leif Hetland (a Middle East country). This number does not include the scores of thousands saved in Brazil as a result of the Toronto revival. Neither does it include the evangelistic fruit of the continued ministry of Howard-Browne, nor that of the Brownsville/Pensacola Revival or the Smithton Revival. I can only speak personally to some of the fruit I am aware of that is related to what happened in and through those who were impacted by the outpouring of the Spirit in Toronto.

One Mighty Rushing River

I believe these revivals that occurred during the last decade of the 20th century were not, in actuality, multiple revivals, but rather were one mighty move of God. In a similar way, the Great Evangelical Revival in England and the First Great Awakening in the United States were both part of one major move of God. The same is true for the Second Great Awakening that broke out throughout the United States and for the mid-19th-century revivals in America, England, Scotland, the Hebrides Island of Lewis, and other locations. The great Holiness-Pentecostal Revival that began near the end of the 19th century and continued into the first decade of the 20th century occurred simultaneously in several countries and continents at the same time, as did the revivals in 1947, 1948, 1949, and 1952. None of these were scattered revivals, in my opinion, but were expressions of one mighty move of God during that time.

Two thousand years ago, a handful of men gave their lives for the spread of the Gospel. They walked and lived beside God in the flesh, and when He sent His precious Holy Spirit, they received it without hesitation. On the Day of Pentecost, after the Holy Spirit had fallen on those assembled,

> *"Some, however, made fun of them and said, 'They have had too much wine.' Then Peter stood up with the Eleven, raised his voice and addressed the crowd: '...In the last days, God says, I will pour out My Spirit on all people...I will show wonders in the heaven above and signs on the earth below"* (Acts 2:13,17,19 NIV).

A little later, after the healing of the crippled beggar, Peter again addresses the naysayers:

> *"The God of Abraham, Isaac and Jacob, the God of our fathers, has glorified his servant Jesus." "... Repent, then, and turn to God, so that your sins may be wiped out, that times of refreshing may come from the Lord, and that he may send the Messiah, who has been appointed for you—even Jesus"* (Acts 3:13,19-20 NIV).

The time of God's refreshing is always available to us. How are we to receive such a great gift such as the Holy Spirit when He comes to us? Just as Jesus did—with prayer and thanksgiving for every opportunity to give glory to God. Imagine the Church fully embracing the presence and power of God. Nothing could contain such an explosive power of Heaven. Without God's power working within us, we are always and everywhere out of our spiritual depth.

But with Him, all things are possible. The good people of God whom I have labored beside for many years in ministry are not extremists. While they may often seek the extreme presence of God, they seek it from a place of balance and spiritual maturity. They are willing to risk it all for Jesus because they know Him intimately. Rather than fearing His presence and power, they earnestly desire these things for the work of ministry. They are willing to fall down, shake, roll, weep, and cry out for God if it means getting up with a greater capacity to love like Jesus and the power to resist sin in their lives. They are possessed with an unquenchable hunger and thirst for more of God. They run toward the source of the power of the risen Jesus Christ so that they may know Him better and make

Him known. They seek the Giver, not the gifts, and above all else, they seek His heart of love.

The Quest for More

Two of the people who most exemplify this quest for the *more* of God are John and Carol Arnott. This is why I highly commend them and this book to you. These aren't leaders I've studied at a distance. We were in the *fire* together. Quite literally, we ministered side by side in the middle of revival for days, weeks, months and years. We've pressed in together on a mutual pursuit: to determine how an outpouring of the Spirit can be sustained and stewarded unto increase.

So I invite you, please, take what's written in these pages seriously. Go back, review, and meditate on what John and Carol shared, as what they've offered you is not revival theory, it's revival fact. What they did to position themselves for more of God, you can do too. The Arnotts positioned themselves to experience and steward a "suddenly" move of the Spirit that has impacted the planet. They did and are continuing to do a great job of stewarding this move of God whose ripple effects are still being felt. They are two humble, loving, pure, and authentic vessels of the Lord who still seem overwhelmed that the Holy Spirit dramatically visited their little church at the end of the Toronto runway back in January 1994. It's this awe and wonder that, I believe, makes them fit candidates to steward what God did *then* and what He is preparing to do. So I ask, *Are you prepared for what God is preparing?*

In the 1980s and early '90s there was a recurring prophecy that a great move of God's Spirit was coming. It would actually be in two waves. The first wave would come to the Church, bringing renewal to the Church, setting it on fire and bringing back the backsliders. The second wave would be to the streets, bringing in a harvest of lost souls. I believe that Toronto and the other outpourings of the mid-90s were the fulfillment of the first wave. I believe we are positioned to feel the swelling of the next wave to the lost.

As we stand on the edge of God's revival fire burning around the world in the 21st century, will we continue to be offended when God shows up in ways that confound our natural minds, or will we be courageous enough to reach out and take hold of our birthright as believers? Will we remain open to observe and examine the fruit, as Jonathan Edwards recommended? I encourage you to seek Him and let His love overtake you—then watch where it takes you.

RANDY CLARK, DMIN.
President and Founder, Global Awakening
Bestselling author of *There is More* and
The Essential Guide to Healing and *Baptized in the Spirit*

Prophetic Words about the Next Wave of Holy Spirit Outpouring

Barbara Yoder
January 17, 2014

I believe that we have entered a new era, greater than a season or phase. And there is yet something that is to happen that will ignite this next period of history that we have entered. I believe it is heralding an all-new age. We are being set up for it. And there is a spiritual empowerment at the door that will cause us to soar above our enemies; it may just perhaps be the beginning of the countdown to Jesus's return. And the remnant will be overtaken with His glory....

It is like nothing we have experienced before. There is such an ethereal, heavenly quality to it, yet totally accessible to the hungry, serious seeker. It is like we are going to punch through that final, very thin by now membrane between Heaven and earth. Heaven will be released on earth to the remnant in an unusual and astounding manner. The miraculous will seem ordinary, yet we will fall on our faces at the manifestation of it for it will be His manifest presence and glory. Holiness will break out and great joyful repentance will begin to roll down like a glorious river.

New resources and supply are going to be multiplied like the woman Elisha told to get the bottles to fill. He will fill all the bottles we bring Him, so it's a time for big faith. Find every bottle we can and then more because the only limitation will be the number of bottles we bring Him. From the heart, not the mind. To the abandoned givers in every realm, miraculous, amazing supply is going to be released.

It is the day of the childlike spirit, full of wonder and awe, expectation and simplicity, from a heart of simple abandoned love and trust—childlike love and trust.

There will be a breaking out of His supernatural love among the true Body like never before. We will be like family, closer than natural family, and even that will be supernatural. God has been dealing with the orphan spirit because it separates us, causes us to move out of competition and striving to prove our worth and significance. It is time to truly come home, come home to Him fully and to His assigned place for us; the love and covenant commitment will be greater than even our natural homes.

I honestly believe a whole new movement that will ultimately usher in the second coming is going to be released. It is going to be like a snowball that starts rolling, gains both size and momentum. I hear, "Don't try to contain or organize it because it has a momentum all its own that is truly fueled by Heaven's mandate." It has everything to do with the launching of the true New Testament church dynamic that will advance beyond anything we have thought or imagined.

Presence, God's manifest presence in and among us. and *exousia* will mark the day, not *dunamis*. *Dunamis* will flow out of God's presence among us and the corresponding revelation of *exousia*, our legal right to legislate Heaven on earth because we are people of the presence, His presence. In the presence will be the outbreak of His glory.

A caution I have been sensing has to do with how we handle the size and movement of what we are moving into. I have heard the word "flotilla" again and again. Build flotillas, not huge organizations, for the administration must serve the movement and not vice versa. The temptation will be to develop administration and organization in a way that will ultimately stop the move of God. And the leaders must be apostolic visionaries who will fearlessly lead us into new territory and models that will accelerate the movement, not slow it down nor stop it....

I was a product (not present at the time) of one of the greatest outpourings in 1948 that went on for five years. I gleaned much from that, particularly an apostolic and prophetic spirit fueled by God's presence. It eventually dissipated (took years to happen) because they kept trying to recapture what was and secondly passed the leadership to the next generation, giving it to a gifted apostolic teacher and CEO type whose passion was organizational and administrative, eventually killing the "movement."

So all of this to say, I believe we are sitting on the edge of a brand-new move of God which will have, of course, familiar elements but a whole new explosive manifestation of God's presence and ultimately empowerment, including new calls, etc., etc. that will thrust us into the final and greatest harvest earth has ever experienced, preparing the way for Jesus's return.

Chuck Pierce
January 24, 2014

What an honor to be a part of the more of the spirit that energized and renewed us over the last 20 years.

I hear the Lord saying,

"A new move has begun.
You have stayed the course of the river
until now, but now you will open a flood
gate that was closed in the last season.
This will produce a torrent.
This next move will come from the mountain.
This move will connect with Zion.
This move will produce new weapons for new wars.
This move will accelerate into new places.
Receive and wear this mantle for the next 17 years!"

About John and Carol Arnott

JOHN AND CAROL ARNOTT ARE THE FOUNDING PASTORS OF CATCH the Fire—formerly known as the Toronto Airport Christian Fellowship—and overseers of the Partners in Harvest Network of Churches. As international speakers, John and Carol have become known for their ministry of revival in the context of the Father's saving and restoring love. As the Holy Spirit moves with signs and wonders, they have seen millions of lives touched and changed through God's power and Christ's love.

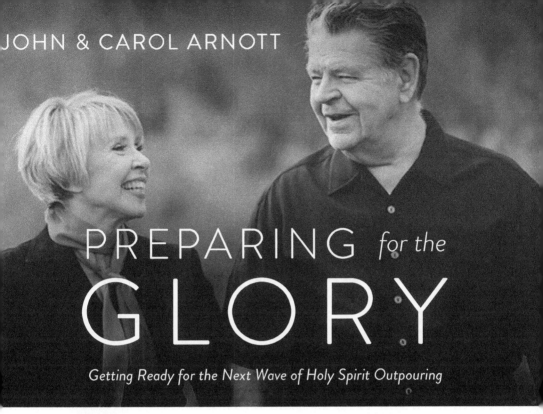

JOHN & CAROL ARNOTT

PREPARING *for the*
GLORY

Getting Ready for the Next Wave of Holy Spirit Outpouring

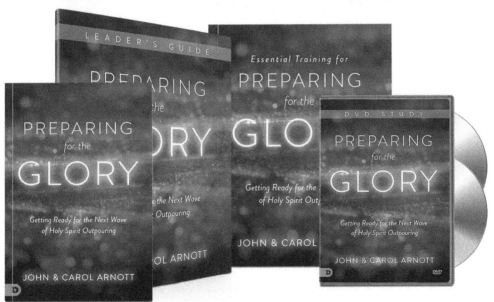

FREE E-BOOKS?
YES, PLEASE!

Get **FREE** and deeply discounted **Christian books** for your **e-reader** delivered to your inbox **every week!**

IT'S SIMPLE!

VISIT lovetoreadclub.com

SUBSCRIBE by entering your email address

RECEIVE free and discounted e-book offers and inspiring articles delivered to your inbox every week!

Unsubscribe at any time.

SUBSCRIBE NOW!

LOVE TO READ CLUB

visit **LOVETOREADCLUB.COM** ▶

CPSIA information can be obtained
at www.ICGtesting.com
Printed in the USA
BVHW01*2253110318
510178BV00008B/233/P